AF767586

SWITCH THINKING

A simple yet powerful guide to changing how you think. Dr Ken Hudson shows how small mindset shifts can unlock creativity, energy and fresh perspectives exactly when you need them. You will use these approaches every day.

Professor Anne Bamford, OBE FCGI Director
International Research Agency, President Education
Inspiring Peace Laboratory

There is something incredibly empowering about realizing you don't need more time or resources to think more creatively. You simply need to switch. In *Switch Thinking,* Dr. Ken Hudson provides a compelling and practical framework for doing just that. His focus on small, intentional shifts in thinking, especially in the middle of real-world moments, resonates strongly with the work we need to do in education and leadership today. This book is a thoughtful and accessible guide to becoming more agile, creative, and responsive in how we think and act.

Cyndi Burnett, Ed.D, Director of Possibilities,
Creativity and Education

In a world of constant information, switch thinking teaches us to pause, switch, and then play with another way of thinking about the current situation or problem. Dr Ken Hudson provides a guide for how to successfully bring different thinking into situations to get better outcomes.

Adjunct Professor Greg Joffe,
Nous Group and University of NSW

Switch Thinking is a must-read for anyone seeking to be more productive, more creative and more innovative in everything they do. Truly groundbreaking.

Paul D. Leinberger,
Ph.D., co-author, *Unfiltered Marketing*

Dr Ken Hudson used his Switch Thinking approach to help me see both the problems and the opportunities in my business in a totally new light. That insight probably saved my business.

Peter Wilson, small business owner

Ken Hudson has written a highly practical guide to one of the most valuable capabilities in a fast-moving world: the ability to shift your thinking in real time. *Switch Thinking* is clear, engaging and full of tools that help people unlock fresh perspective, energy and possibility. What I like most is that it is not just interesting, it is usable. This is a book with ideas you can apply immediately in leadership, teamwork, problem solving and everyday life.

Graham Winter, organisational psychologist,
bestselling author of *Think One Team*

SWITCH THINKING

THE 2-MINUTE SWITCH TO BOOST YOUR CREATIVITY, ENERGY AND FOCUS

DR KEN HUDSON

WILEY

First published 2026 by John Wiley & Sons Australia, Ltd

© The Original Thinking Company Pty Ltd, 2026

All rights reserved, including rights for text and data mining and training of artificial intelligence technologies or similar technologies. Except as permitted under the *Australian Copyright Act 1968* (for example, a fair dealing for the purposes of study, research, criticism or review) no part of this publication may be reproduced, stored in a retrieval system, or transmitted, in any form or by any means, electronic, mechanical, photocopying, recording or otherwise. Advice on how to obtain permission to reuse material from this title is available at http://www.wiley.com/go/permissions.

The right of Dr Ken Hudson to be identified as the author of *Switch Thinking* has been asserted in accordance with law.

ISBN: 978-1-394-44523-3

NATIONAL LIBRARY OF AUSTRALIA

A catalogue record for this book is available from the National Library of Australia

Registered Office
John Wiley & Sons Australia, Ltd. Level 4, 600 Bourke Street, Melbourne, VIC 3000, Australia

For details of our global editorial offices, customer services, and more information about Wiley products visit us at www.wiley.com.

Wiley also publishes its books in a variety of electronic formats and by print-on-demand. Some content that appears in standard print versions of this book may not be available in other formats.

Trademarks: Wiley and the Wiley logo are trademarks or registered trademarks of John Wiley & Sons, Inc. and/or its affiliates in the United States and other countries and may not be used without written permission. All other trademarks are the property of their respective owners. John Wiley & Sons, Inc. is not associated with any product or vendor mentioned in this book.

Limit of Liability/Disclaimer of Warranty
While the publisher and author have used their best efforts in preparing this work, they make no representations or warranties with respect to the accuracy or completeness of the contents of this work and specifically disclaim all warranties, including without limitation any implied warranties of merchantability or fitness for a particular purpose. No warranty may be created or extended by sales representatives, written sales materials or promotional statements for this work. This work is sold with the understanding that the publisher is not engaged in rendering professional services. The advice and strategies contained herein may not be suitable for your situation. You should consult with a specialist where appropriate. The fact that an organisation, website, or product is referred to in this work as a citation and/or potential source of further information does not mean that the publisher and author endorse the information or services the organisation, website, or product may provide or recommendations it may make. Further, readers should be aware that websites listed in this work may have changed or disappeared between when this work was written and when it is read. Neither the publisher nor author shall be liable for any loss of profit or any other commercial damages, including but not limited to special, incidental, consequential, or other damages.

Cover design by Wiley

Set in 11.5/16.5 pts and Warnock Pro by Straive, Chennai, India.
Printed and bound by CPI Group (UK) Ltd, Croydon, CR0 4YY

C9781394445233_080826

The manufacturer's authorized representative according to the EU General Product Safety Regulation is Wiley-VCH GmbH, Boschstr. 12, 69469 Weinheim, Germany,
e-mail: Product_Safety@wiley.com.

This book is dedicated to the people who inspire me every day,
Margot, Molly and Charlotte.

Contents

About the author

Dr Ken Hudson has a B Bus (UTS), an MBA (UNE) and a PhD (UWS). His PhD thesis was 'Designing a continuously creative organization'.

Dr Hudson is the author of three internationally released books: *The Idea Generator, The Idea Accelerator* and *Speed Thinking* (all published by Allen & Unwin).

Ken was a part-time lecturer for more than 10 years at the University of Technology, Sydney. In his corporate life he was a marketing director at American Express and held senior positions at Citibank and Dunlop Slazenger as well as in advertising.

In his consulting role, Ken has worked with leaders of some of the biggest brands in Australia and Asia, helping them to think differently, solve complex problems and develop breakthrough innovations.

Q. In a rapidly changing world,
what is the quality you need more than ever?

A. The ability to change your thinking.

Otherwise, you will be left behind.

Introduction: Pause — Switch — Play

Let's consider this situation.

You are making a presentation to a group of senior managers. You start well, outline the topic, why it's important and what you will cover. You have prepared well and are on top of your content. There is a flow to your slides. You are on fire but then …

Halfway through, a hand goes up and one of the leaders asks you an unexpected question.

Here are two scenarios as to what happens next:

- *Scenario A:* You get flustered, nervous and hesitant. Despite your preparation, you had not anticipated this question. You start to repeat yourself and refer to your slides for inspiration. You are stuck, your mind goes blank and you start to feel the frustration in the room.
- *Scenario B:* You effortlessly switch your thinking and depart from the written text for a few moments asking the group to answer this question from a customer — rather than a business — perspective. What are our customers thinking, feeling and doing when they interact with us? You see and feel nods from the group.

Hopefully you relate more to scenario B. But, unfortunately, I have experienced scenario A more times than I care to remember both as a presenter, leader, university lecturer and observer.

The difference between the two scenarios is not intelligence, confidence or preparation. It's the ability to switch your thinking. And more particularly the ability to switch in real time…

This morning I checked my various social media feeds for what is happening in the world. Then I clicked on a few of my favourite apps, which update and curate my news feeds.

My point?

This all happened in real time.

And yet, our thinking has not kept pace with the speed and volume of information we receive constantly. It's why we often get stuck: there is a time lag between information and thinking. Problems emerge in real time and most of these can and should be solved in real time. This is why Switch Thinking is so empowering. You can use it right now. Just pause, switch and play for 2 minutes and you have invariably created a new possibility or solution, or at the very least seen a situation differently. Switch Thinking elevates your creativity, agility and confidence in real time. Think of it as an energy boost for your mind.

You might ask, 'How are we solving this problem now?'

Switch.

You could also ask, 'How might we solve this problem in three years' time?'

When you ask 'How are we solving this problem now?' you are asking for understanding, explanation and improvement. This is valuable and important.

However, when you ask 'How might we solve this problem in three years' time?' you are asking a very different question. You are imagining a desirable future result, goal or experience. Often this simple change in language can unlock a burst of creativity and energy.

Both questions are valid. And you can switch back and forth between the two, and perhaps even try to connect some ideas from each question to develop a bigger solution.

The Switch Thinking focus: 'During'

Switch Thinking has a focus that is different from and has long been ignored by other approaches to learning, change, growth, performance and development.

As illustrated in figure I.1, the focus is on 'during'.

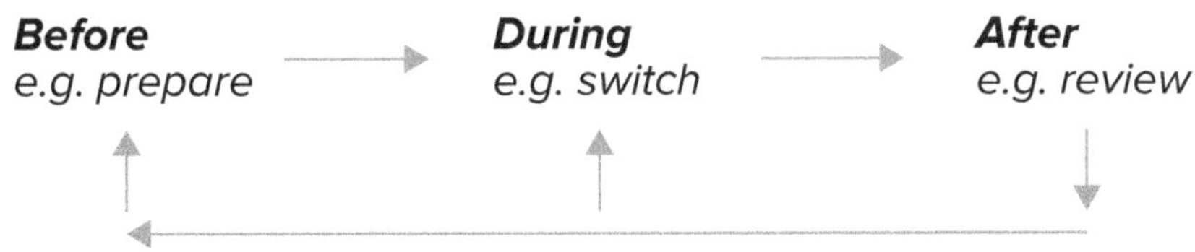

Figure I.1 The Switch Thinking focus is on 'during'

In any performance, change or experience (e.g. a meeting or an interview) there is a *before*, a *during* and an *after*.

The *before* might consist of preparing, planning, visualising or role playing.

The *after* might involve reviewing, coaching, mentoring or journalling.

These are all important.

But what about the *during* phase?

This is where Switch Thinking can help you perform at your best. Most importantly, it's often when you need Switch Thinking the most.

The switches and prompts of Switch Thinking can help you 'during' any conversation, whether that be a leadership, parental or feedback interaction. It gives you a way to escape your automatic mode of thinking and explore a new approach for a few minutes.

For example, when leading a monthly team meeting, your usual approach could be, 'What are the facts, figures, numbers, trends, gaps?'

Switch.

'How is everyone feeling?'

Notice how you have switched the focus of the discussion from profits to people. And this happened in an instant. By doing so, you now have a much broader and often more insightful way of looking at your team's performance. In this example you have switched your (and others') thinking in a deliberate, proactive way.

You don't have to wait for an unexpected question to switch. You can use Switch Thinking at any time; in any situation; with a group, team or AI. In a world of declining attention spans, limited time and rapid change, you literally only have moments to create a positive impression, connect with others or create a new possibility.

This is why Switch Thinking revolves around a 2-minute time frame—because often that is all the time you have. It's a real-time thinking system for a real-time world.

The great news is that you don't need to learn how to be more creative, energised or focused. You already have these abilities. Switch Thinking can show you how to activate these based on how your brain is already operating. All you need is a few switches and a couple of minutes.

And the results are immediate. A switch in thinking can lead to a switch in how you feel and what you do. And the effect can be exponential, as you can see in figure I.2.

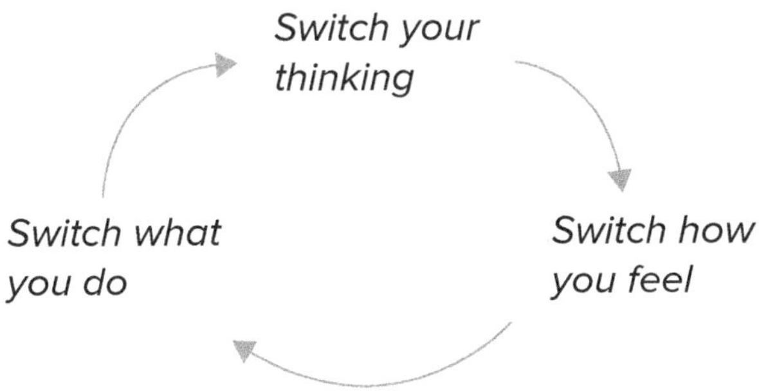

Figure I.2 Switch Thinking cycle
Source: Inspired by S. Edelman (2002), *Change your Thinking*, Sydney, ABC Books

My insight

The inspiration for Switch Thinking came from watching a bilingual colleague at a conference in Singapore switch seamlessly between English and Mandarin. This was a learned skill, I reminded myself. I wondered, could you do the same thing with your thinking—for example, switching back and forth between logic and imagination, reason and emotion, or analysis and intuition?

Through trial and error, and testing with thousands of people I have found that anyone can learn Switch Thinking easily and quickly. And most importantly, you can start using it immediately with confidence.

You can switch to a different mode of thinking exactly when you need to. I call this Ball Mode and as the name suggests it is creative, fun and playful. You can also switch back to your usual mode of thinking, which I call Box Mode (i.e. structured and analytical). The switch is not permanent. It's like switching to a new television channel, seeing what is on and if you don't like anything, then you switch back. The most you have lost is 2 minutes.

With Switch Thinking you have agency, choice, control and flexibility. You can switch your thinking anytime, anywhere, with anyone.

Pause — Switch — Play (PSP)

The core of Switch Thinking is PSP (Pause, Switch, Play).

It's an easily remembered, three-step mnemonic that captures the essence of the Switch Thinking approach.

PSP.

Pause — Switch — Play.

It's short, rhythmical, sequential and action-based. The three verbs tell you what to do. It's a cognitive script you can use anytime, with anyone, in any situation. You can use PSP at work, home, college, school and everywhere in between.

Use it enough and it becomes automatic over time.

Pause

Pause is the space between stimulus and response.

You pause for a few seconds as you realise that your current approach is not working or that a new approach might pay dividends. Or something has changed.

It's a way to interrupt your usual thinking and gives you agency, choice and control. You might pause for one breath, and take a second breath before responding or to notice what is really happening.

Switch

Now switch your thinking.

You switch from your default mode of thinking to a different mode. Typically this is from Box Mode to Ball Mode, but not always. Think of switching a light switch on or off. A simple switch can change a situation instantly. Now imagine if you had the same power over your thinking.

It does not matter what you switch. It could be the question, perspective, focus or an assumption (in the second half of the book I outline 6 switches that can help you switch your thinking). The key point is that you are escaping your established thinking patterns. In this one, cognitive movement you are exploring a new direction.

You can leap from stuck to unstuck in an instant.

Play

Now play and explore this new switch in thinking for 2 minutes or less. Give yourself permission to explore a new direction without filtering. It's liberating, creative and empowering. You can play and feel safe because you know you can always return to your usual way of thinking.

Here's an example.

The situation: You have been given a new project at work.

Pause: You feel disengaged and bored with this new assignment.

Switch: Now you switch.

Play: In this case, you switch your perspective to a magician. Why a magician? Who cares, it doesn't matter. It was the first thing that entered your consciousness, so why not keep going with it? You now ask yourself, Where is the drama? The mystery? The sleight of hand?

You start playing with this new perspective.

Suddenly your mind lights up. You are filled with new notions. In just a few minutes you are flooded with new ideas, possibilities and energy. You are full of surprises as you have disrupted your existing thinking patterns. And the good news is that you can return to your usual way of thinking at any time. It is an exciting yet safe journey.

Figure I.3 illustrates the three-step PSP process.

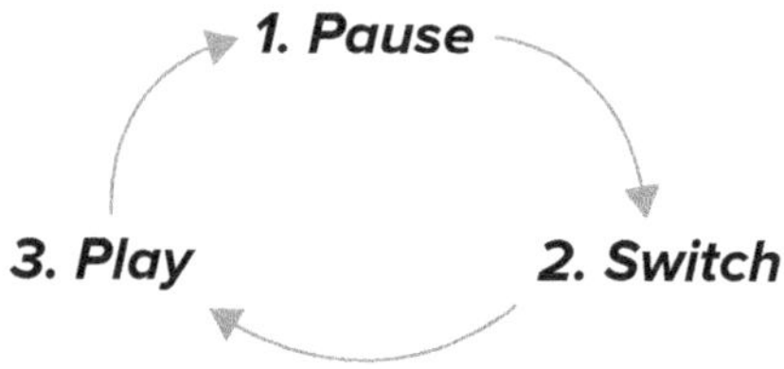

Figure I.3 The Pause—Switch—Play process

When you have experienced the three-step Pause—Switch—Play process and you experience the results you look forward to using it again.

With PSP you now have a cognitive trigger. Elite sportspeople often have a trigger physical movement to help them get ready for the next point or ball. In cricket, for example, a batsman might move back and across in their stance before the bowler lets the ball go. This engages them physically and mentally to switch on their full concentration.

I use the words *pause, switch* and *play* in a similar way but as a thinking trigger. PSP is a fast, simple and easy way to change your thinking when you are under pressure. Repeated use of pause, switch and play as thinking triggers strengthens your neural network.

Consider this example.

The situation: You are leading a team that is trying to solve a challenging problem.
Pause: You realise that your business-as-usual solutions are not working as they have in the past.
Switch: What are some impossible solutions?
Play: Let's play with these types of impossible solutions for a few minutes and see where they take us.

This is a simple switch in thinking that can impact how the team feel about this problem (i.e. anything is possible). It can re-energise any group and potentially help you develop transformative ideas using a simple switch in thinking.

> Repeat the words 'Pause—Switch—Play' slowly out loud to yourself six times in 30 seconds.
>
> Get used to using the rhythm of this three-word process! Your goal is to develop a new, neural switch pattern in your brain and be able to use this process in a natural, comfortable way.

When you are presented with a new idea:

Pause: You usually ask, Why?
Switch: Ask, Why not?
Play: Have fun with this new idea. Why not give it a go? Find reasons why it will work; try to enhance the initial idea in five different ways in 2 minutes.

The 'why' question can be useful though it's often critical and accusing. Asking 'why not', by comparison, is open, inviting and motivating. Both are valid but notice how the Pause—Switch—Play process can create a very different experience.

The aim of this book

My goal with this book is to help you develop your Switch Thinking skill so it becomes second nature. By doing so you can lead your life with more creativity, energy and agility.

You really have more control over your thinking than you realise. This insight is for many people almost a revolutionary idea. You may have a preference for a particular mode of thinking but that is all it is: a preference. You can switch.

My other goal is to help you showcase this wonderful ability to others. I have tried to make the language, metaphors, switches, prompts and examples varied and real life so that you can communicate, role model and teach others how to switch whenever they wish.

Switch Thinking is a powerful way to escape the status quo and make a big impact in minutes. As one participant in a Switch Thinking workshop volunteered, 'It's like you are tricking your brain into changing without using the word change'.

How to read this book

I have learned that the best way to develop your Switch Thinking skill is by doing, not just reading. Hence, I have tried to make this book both practical and thought provoking, with numerous examples, diagrams, prompts and exercises. You can come back to these again and again.

You can read Switch Thinking in any order. If you are in a hurry, flip to one of the 6 switches in chapters 7 to 12 and start generating new possibilities in the next few minutes. Just start switching. There is no right or wrong way to switch. Play with any of the switches or prompts, write your ideas in the margin or start using the word 'switch' in your conversations with others.

In Appendix A at the back of the book, you will find suggestions for wonderful ADHD minds. For people with ADHD, creativity tends not to be an issue, hence switching to more structure, even for a few minutes, can be hugely beneficial.

Real-life application

Some years ago, my wife and I employed a promising young architect to design our new house. In our meetings, we found ourselves bogged down in technical details. The architect was operating in what I call Box Mode and ignored our fears, hopes and dreams for our new home.

Sensing this, in the next meeting our architect switched to Ball Mode and built a model of his design out of matchsticks. Suddenly, we could see, feel and touch our new house. We were sold!

All it required was a simple switch.

• • •

Switch Thinking is empowering, energising and transforming. Are you ready to begin your journey?

Chapter 1

A quick overview of Switch Thinking

For a short while, I worked in a mid-size advertising agency. I loved working with clients on their business problems. Although I was new to the industry, having worked on the client side for some time, I was soon indoctrinated to the importance of gaining new business.

Out of all the new business pitches I was involved with I remember one in particular. Our pitch document was beautifully put together, the pitch team had rehearsed numerous times, and the advertising strategy and solution were sound. We were prepared and ready.

And yet, halfway through our presentation I sensed that the client had some reservations. Their body language gave it away. I jumped in and asked them, 'How did you feel about the ideas we were presenting?' This gave the client a space to raise their concerns.

Rather than argue, or defend our current advertising strategy, I said that I agreed with many of the issues they had raised (much to the surprise and perhaps consternation of our CEO). 'We need some new thinking', I continued, 'and if you give us a week we can come back to you with a new approach'.

A week later we did in fact develop and present a new strategy and were delighted to hear that we had won the pitch. The client was impressed not only with the new thinking and our agility but most importantly, she said, that we had the courage during the presentation to pause and be open to changing our approach.

I tell this story not to highlight my role but to give you a glimpse of how Switch Thinking works.

The what, why, when, where, who and how of Switch Thinking

The '5 Ws and H' is a fabulous framework to describe Switch Thinking. In doing so, I hope to answer many of your questions. This, then, frees you up to explore and play with the processes, switches and prompts of this approach.

What is Switch Thinking?

I define Switch Thinking as the skill of knowing when — and how — to change the way you think, feel and act.

It's the skill of being able to switch your thinking in 2-minute bursts exactly when you need to. This is a skill you can develop, practise and improve, much like learning to play the guitar, playing pickleball or driving a car.

You start small, try a switch, see what happens, feel the impact and before you know it what seemed impossible is now an everyday experience.

Switch Thinking is the ability to switch your thinking between two different modes (i.e. Box Mode and Ball Mode) based on the situation, challenge, moment or need. It connects the latest developments in brain science, neuroplasticity and the processing power of AI. It can mean switching between different modes of thinking (more on this later), the individual and the group and even between humans and AI.

Switch Thinking can be used by anyone, anytime, anywhere. You do not have to wait for the right people, space, place or mood.

I have found that when you switch, the impact is direct, and often exponential, as people see a situation in a new way. When you develop your Switch Thinking skill you can think on your feet, avoid procrastination and feel less anxious. When you know how to switch, your life can change, one moment at a time.

This switching between different modes of thinking is the essence of Switch Thinking. It's what your brain is doing automatically. The good news is that much of what I suggest in this book might emulate approaches that you are already taking intuitively. For example, you can switch the conversation at a dinner party; or switch your hairstyle, outfit, channels — or lanes when you are driving. These are instances where you realise your current approach needs to change so you proactively make a change. Switch Thinking is similar, but the switch is applied to your thinking.

Why is Switch Thinking needed more than ever?

We tend to think in patterns. These neural patterns have been built up over the years, so they are established and quickly accessible. This makes our thinking efficient, comfortable and predictable. Our thinking patterns are typically based on what has worked in the past.

According to the latest brain science, there are two different networks we use to create, solve, decide, and so on. I have suggested two metaphors to describe the workings of these two brain networks. I call these Box Mode and Ball Mode. As the names suggest, these metaphors describe two different ways to think, feel and act. Box Mode is more structured, and Ball Mode is more creative. Most people prefer one mode or the other — or at least start in a particular mode.

Most people have learned that a particular mode is typically well suited for their environment. In a corporate working environment — with its emphasis on budgets, goals, project management and key performance indicators — it's no surprise that being in Box Mode is an advantage.

On the other hand, in a more free-wheeling culture — say, a design, film, advertising agency or playing with your kids at home — starting in Ball Mode might be beneficial. This is the key point. This is your starting mode — although you can switch modes whenever you need to.

This matching of thinking modes to the situation, culture or team environment makes perfect sense. And sticking to your starting or preferred thinking mode is understandable because it has worked for you in the past and you feel comfortable and confident using it.

There are, however, two problems with this approach (this is the 'why' of Switch Thinking).

The first problem arises when your preferred specific mode becomes the dominant one. If you are stuck for a new idea, then more Box Mode analysis may not lead to a creative breakthrough. You need to switch, even for a few minutes, to Ball Mode.

Likewise, if you have a beautiful ADHD mind you can feel overwhelmed with ideas, ruminating or procrastinating, then a switch to Box Mode to move forward with a specific, concrete action is the order of the day.

The second problem is that due to dwindling attention spans, the pace of change and the focus on results, moments matter. You often get judged not on the rigour of your hour-long presentation but on the 30 seconds when you answered an unexpected question. The problem is that under pressure in these moments, you tend to default to the mode you are most comfortable being in. If this is Box Mode, then you revert to more Box Mode. If you prefer Ball Mode, you tend to stay in this mode.

In key moments this means you become more rigid rather than displaying the greater creativity and agility that the moment calls for. And many of us fail to perform at the level that we usually do in these moments.

This is not due to a lack of preparation, commitment or interest. It's simply using your default thinking mode regardless of the moment.

It is for these reasons that being able to switch your thinking is so important in a changing, uncertain environment. Past thinking is helpful as a guide, but it should not be a straitjacket.

When should you use Switch Thinking?

You can use Switch Thinking at any time, at work, at home, in a café, by yourself, with friends or with AI. Any time you need to change the way you think, feel and act.

I have found, however, that Switch Thinking really comes alive in two quite different situations.

1. *When you realise that your current approach isn't working.* For example:

   - a conversation with your partner suddenly turns tense or emotional
   - you don't feel that you are being heard at a dinner party
   - your team leader wants to discuss your latest results
   - you are feeling increasingly nervous in an interview.

   Switch Thinking works really well in these circumstances because it can help you escape your default way of thinking and switch to a new way—instantly. This means you (and others) can get unstuck, free your mind from past patterns and explore new opportunities. Most importantly, it can help you in the moment. When you are right in the thick of things and your performance is on the line.

   You might have been asked by a colleague to give some feedback about a presentation they just made that didn't go well. You are in Box Mode and start talking about structure, typefaces or even a spelling mistake on slide 7, which makes the situation worse.

However, all your colleague wants from you is reassurance that the presentation is not as bad as they think. You pause and switch to Ball Mode for a few minutes to reassure, listen and rebuild confidence.

2. *When you (or others) need something new quickly.*
   It could be a new way of seeing a situation — perhaps a new insight, idea or solution. Or it could be a new practical step forward.

Switch Thinking, with its two modes and array of switches, prompts and innovative ways of working with AI gives you and others a toolkit to think differently. You do not have to wait for a brainstorming, ideation or problem-solving session. You can create often effective new possibilities in minutes. All you need is to switch.

Where can you use Switch Thinking?

Switch Thinking is a meta skill — like listening. This means that you can use it anywhere, anytime, with anyone. You do not need a special breakout room, laptop or smartphone. Use it whenever you wish. There are no rules. In my workshops I often have to (seemingly) give people permission to switch their thinking whenever they wish, wherever they are.

It's your mind, your thinking, your choice.

You can switch your thinking at work, at home, on the sporting field, in the classroom or in a lecture hall. It is not bound by a physical time, space or place.

I love that Switch Thinking can be used in a subtle way to change the direction of a conversation without the other person realising what is happening. This gives you greater control and agency to steer a conversation in whatever direction you wish.

Or you can use Switch Thinking in a more explicit way. For example, you might say to a group, team or partner, 'Why don't we switch our thinking and think of five questions about this problem that we have not asked before in the next few minutes?'

I have found that Switch Thinking can be used with kids, with experts, and with everyone in between. Everyone gets stuck or fixated on their default thinking mode, meaning they can benefit from an implicit or explicit switch.

Let's look at another situation.

The situation: You are meeting a potential client or employer for the first time.

Your preferred mode is Box Mode as you start to talk about your position, role, experiences, qualifications and so on.

Pause: You pause. This approach is not working.

Switch: You switch to Ball Mode. Now you start playing in Ball Mode for a few minutes.

Play: You ask them first about their business, needs or goals. You listen intently. You might ask about their pain points or recent wins. After a few minutes you switch back to Box Mode to build reassurance, competency and capability.

This switch in thinking can also flow from Ball Mode to Box Mode…

A few years ago, I was working with a successful advertising agency in a new business idea session, and they were literally drowning in ideas (i.e. they were operating in Ball Mode).

Pause.

'What if we switched to Box Mode?' I suggested as they struggled with what ideas might offer the best return.

'What ideas can we test in the next 90 days?' I asked.

Within minutes, the group had decided on their top three ideas. This provided a much-needed focus for the next hour the group spent on this challenge.

Who can use Switch Thinking?

I have introduced Switch Thinking to adults, kids, engineers, sales professionals, small business owners and corporate managers regardless of discipline, function, education or previous experience.

If you have a neurodiverse or a neurotypical mind you can think. And if you can think one way, you can certainly switch to a different way. You might be right-handed, but most of us can still catch a ball with our left hand. Your dominant hand might be stronger, but you can use both hands when required. Your thinking works in a similar way.

Switch Thinking will also appeal to team leaders, coaches, facilitators, trainers, teachers and parents. Anyone who is interested in helping others fulfil their potential and boost their ability to change and perform under pressure. The language is simple, the metaphors are powerful and the idea of switching can be applied to most everyday situations. Most of all, unlike other approaches to change the results are immediate.

Switch Thinking is also easy to role model. You just weave the word 'switch' into any interaction or any leadership, coaching or parental moment. For example, 'Your speech appealed to the head. Perhaps you might switch to more of a heart-based one next time and see what happens'.

As one of my clients said to me, 'I have been trying to encourage greater creativity and innovation in my team for the past 20 years and you are the first person to use the word 'switch' in such a proactive and dynamic way. It's a wonder no-one has thought of it beforehand'.

How does the Switch Thinking system work?

The Switch Thinking system comprises several elements (see figure 1.1). You can use all or some of them in any order.

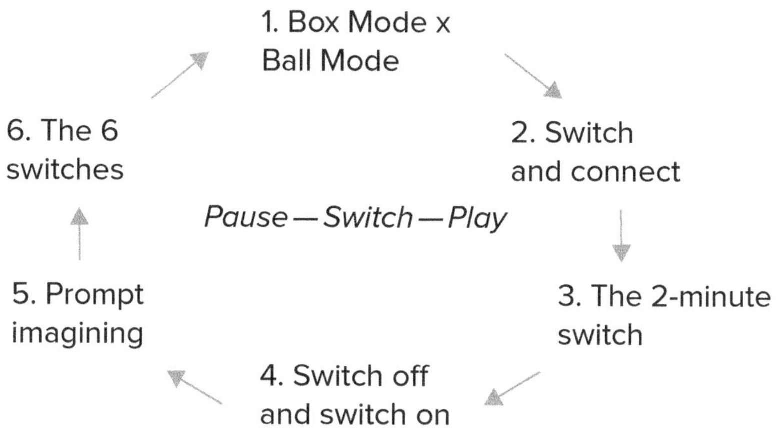

Figure 1.1 Elements of the Switch Thinking system

1 Box Mode × Ball Mode

Switch Thinking is the process of switching back and forth between two different modes of thinking for a few minutes at a time.

As you read earlier, I call these two modes 'Box Mode' and 'Ball Mode'.

Chapter 2 goes into detail about how to operate in either Box Mode or Ball Mode. For now, here is a brief summary of these two powerful metaphors and ways of thinking.

- *Box Mode:* Picture a box in your mind. It's solid, familiar, structured and stable. In brain science it's closely associated with the Central Executive Network (CEN) — a network (note it's not a single hub) responsible for attention, working memory and cognitive control.

  Box Mode is essential for tasks that demand critical thinking, planning and effective execution. It's outward-focused and goal-oriented.

  Box Mode is efficient, safe and comfortable. It houses what has worked before and your assumptions, beliefs, conventions and theories. But it can also keep you trapped in what you have always thought, felt and done.

- *Ball Mode:* Now imagine a ball. What images come to mind? Colour, movement, play and imagination. It's a different mode of thinking. It's not just thinking outside the box, although that is often the effect.

  Ball Mode, as the name suggests, is a completely different way of thinking. It's more free-flowing, unstructured and creative.

  In brain science, a ball metaphor represents your Default Mode Network (DMN). Your DMN kicks in when your mind is at rest (or at least not focused on an external goal directly). It's associated with daydreaming, mind wandering, self-reflection and thinking about the future. Your DMN can help you make unusual and often creative connections and associations.

  For example, meeting a friend for coffee is a wonderful opportunity to switch to Ball Mode (i.e. fun, playful), while having a meeting with your financial advisor about your investments might require a switch to Box Mode (i.e. structured, rational).

Box Mode and Ball Mode are starting modes that you can switch from at any time. Importantly, they are thinking modes, not people. All of us can operate in either mode. I need to stress there is no right or wrong mode. The goal is to match the mode (even for a few minutes) to a moment that matters.

2 Switch and connect

Switching back and forth between Box Mode and Ball Mode is the dynamic action of Switch Thinking. It can help you and others to generate new possibilities when you switch to Ball Mode, and make real, tangible progress when you switch to Box Mode.

But there is also an emergent quality to this switching process when you aim to connect the ideas from both modes. Think of aqua aerobics. It connects swimming and aerobics in a fun, intensive fitness workout.

This is the aim with Switch Thinking. It's not just switching; it's switching and connecting to generate breakthrough ideas and solutions that work.

3 The 2-minute switch

The next element of Switch Thinking is one of the most surprising. It's to switch to a different mode of thinking using any of the 6 switches — but to do it for 2 minutes.

Why 2 minutes?

I have found that if you suggest to people that they switch for only a short time they are more willing to experiment and take a small risk. It's like eating a new entrée rather than a main meal. If it's only 2 minutes, you can always switch back to the usual way.

Switching for 2 minutes is incredibly efficient. There is no time lost on waiting for others or the right time, place or mood. The last point is key: most of us have been taught that we need to be in a flow-like or inspired state to be creative. This makes sense, but what if you need to solve a problem in a hurry? My experience is that the 2-minute time frame helps you unlock your creative thinking right now rather than waiting for this desired state to be available to you.

The 2-minute time frame also switches the pace of your thinking. When ask leaders when they have done their best work, they often say it's when they have no time to overthink or second guess themselves. They just think, feel and act.

Being encouraged to switch your thinking also feels safe — you can always switch back if the new thought pattern doesn't work.

Think of surfing with a leg rope: it's there if you fall off and you can quickly get back on your board. It's adventure within boundaries.

The 2-minute Switch Thinking time frame can be used on any everyday challenge, issue or hiccup. You start with a small switch, gain more confidence and move on to bigger challenges. This means you can develop your Switch Thinking skill step by step rather working on a big challenge right from the start. You are building your Switch Thinking muscle one switch at a time. You are in control; you decide when and where you switch and with whom.

The goal with 2 minutes is frequency, not long, deep meditation or therapy sessions. These are powerful, but Switch Thinking offers a more active, dynamic and complementary approach to other change programs. Think of a short HIIT workout rather than a 3-hour session at the gym. Switch Thinking offers a bite-size way to solve a problem, move forward or disrupt a ruminating pattern of negativity, right here, right now.

4 Switch off and switch on

This is another amazingly simple component of Switch Thinking. It's the idea that you can switch your thoughts off and on. Think of going to the beach and switching off from your work to just be in the moment. Then being able to switch your mind back into work mode when you turn on your laptop.

Let's imagine you can do the same with your thinking.

You deliberately and proactively switch off your automatic thinking pattern and switch on a new mode of thinking for a few minutes and see what happens.

Here's an example.

In the next 2 minutes:

- switch off—logic
- switch on—intuition.

By doing this you are giving yourself and others permission to use and trust their intuition or gut feel, even if it's only for a few minutes.

The switch off and switch on microswitch helps you develop and practise your thinking agility. I have found that this process, when used with the 2-minute time frame, is incredibly effective.

You can use it anywhere, anytime, by yourself, with others or with AI.

5 Prompt imagining

When using AI, most people adopt what is called the 'prompt engineering' approach. The emphasis here is on using prompts that can find, analyse and summarise large bits of information. This approach can be efficient and productive, and saves time on many routine tasks. An example of this kind or prompt would be, *Can you* [ChatGPT] *summarise the five major causes of global warming?* These types of prompts are Box Mode in nature.

Switch Thinking, on the other hand, offers you another, more creative way to use AI. I call this 'prompt imagining'. It's based on the idea that the more creative the prompt, the more creative the AI response. This is more Ball Mode in nature. An example might be, *How might a poet describe the causes of global warming?*

Notice that it's a similar type of question but asked in a more innovative way. This is what I call 'prompt imagining'. The goal is not accuracy, but originality. I have found that using both types of prompts (i.e. engineering and imaginative) can open up your thinking and that of your AI chatbot.

6 The 6 switches

To help you move back and forth between Box Mode and Ball Mode, I have developed and tested what I call the '6 switches'. These are fast, easy and simple.

In the coming chapters I will describe the 6 switches in more detail, but here is a snapshot, just to whet your appetite.

- Switch your perspective (e.g. shift to a dentist perspective).
- Switch your focus (e.g. focus on purpose rather than profit).
- Switch on your imagination (e.g. I wonder …).
- Switch your emotion (e.g. I feel …).
- Switch your rules (e.g. challenge an assumption).
- Switch your questions (e.g. ask a naïve question).

There are no right or wrong switches. And you can use all or some of these, in any order. The 6 switches give you a fast, proactive and deliberate way to switch your thinking. It's a way to explore new possibilities beyond the usual way you think, feel and act.

In the second half of this book you'll find a chapter on each of the 6 switches with prompts for how to use them.

A final point

Most of all, Switch Thinking is about having fun with the way you think. For too long we have considered thinking a serious, deep, time-consuming activity for a chosen few.

But if you switch it around, thinking can be a playful, enjoyable experience that anyone can do, at any time. And most importantly it can be taught, communicated, role-modelled and developed.

A 2-minute Switch Thinking exercise

Practise switching your perspective

With anything new, start small. Perhaps start by switching your perspective—most people in my workshops suggest this is the easiest switch to use.

Pause.

Then switch your perspective.

Ask yourself how a person with a disability, a bored teenager or a retiree might see this situation.

You do not have to tell anyone what you're thinking—just do it as a thought experiment.

There is no right or wrong way to switch. You are just escaping your default mode of thinking for somewhere new. And who knows, you might love playing there.

Again, the outcome does not matter. You are practising switching and in the process you can gain some valuable insights into how others might see the world.

Chapter 2

Box Mode × Ball Mode

As we have seen, in Switch Thinking there are two modes of thinking. I call these Box Mode and Ball Mode. These are metaphors that people find easy to understand and apply. These modes are informed by the latest brain research.

The key point is that these are modes, *not* descriptions of people. This is a liberating and empowering idea because it means you can switch your thinking mode depending on the moment, challenge or preference.

Box Mode is about progress

In my experience, most of us prefer one mode of thinking over another based on what we do, where we work and what has worked in the past. These experiences form efficient neural patterns that can get stronger through repeated use. The good news is, we now know that our brain is far more plastic than we ever imagined, which means we can change its wiring — that is, it's neural patterns.

Let me give you a taste (no pun intended) of how to distinguish between Box Mode and Ball Mode. At a dinner party, a group of friends started talking about the joy of cooking food (for friends on the weekend). Half the group said they followed recipes from their favourite cookbooks (Box Mode), while the other half preferred to experiment with a general idea of the finished meal and whatever food happened to be in the fridge (Ball Mode).

Quick quiz: Do you prefer operating in Box Mode?

For each statement, rate how much you agree:
1 = Strongly disagree
2 = Disagree
3 = Neutral
4 = Agree
5 = Strongly agree

- I like to plan things in detail before I start. __
- I prefer proven methods over untested ideas. __
- I feel most confident when I have clear rules and guidelines. __
- I focus on completing one task before moving on to the next. __
- I prefer step-by-step approaches over experimenting. __

If you scored 15 or more, you probably prefer operating in Box Mode—or, perhaps more accurately, this might represent your starting mode.

What does 'operating in Box Mode' mean?

In your mind, picture a box like the one in figure 2.1.

It is structured, rigid and solid. A box provides order, stability and predictability. It's where your preparation, planning and prioritising takes place. Your box has limits, which ensures you don't venture too far. You can always return to your thinking box when you want to feel safe and secure.

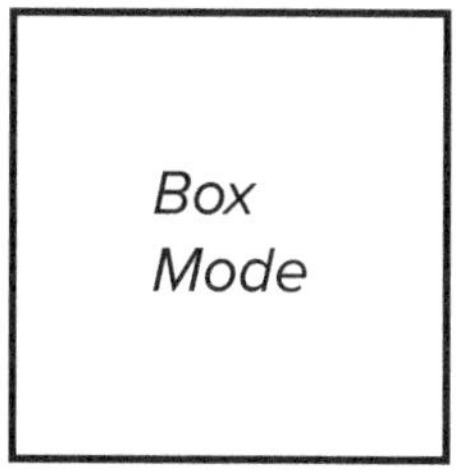

Figure 2.1 Box Mode is essential for tasks that demand critical thinking, planning and effective execution

Operating in Box Mode has a self-reinforcing quality to it. What has worked in the past tends to be repeated, so your thinking can become very efficient but you also run the risk of it becoming increasingly rigid.

Now consider the idea of a box as a metaphor for your thinking. Your Box Mode includes your past experiences, assumptions, theories, models you use and conventions you follow. These inform your goals, ambitions and expectations.

Remember that being in Box Mode is neither good nor bad. It just represents a mode of thinking. The aim is to be aware of what mode you are in at any moment and be willing to switch it if the need arises or the situation changes.

In Box Mode, you tend to cast a critical eye over any new claims, trends or information. You are interested in facts, figures and proof.

For this reason, when giving a presentation I always assume people (at least initially) are in Box Mode. They can be persuaded, but they need research, results or case studies to satisfy their analytical, logical mindset.

Box Mode is the ideal mode for planning, evaluating, prioritising and testing. In this mode you can move from the subjective to the objective; from an idea to concrete action. It's why I call Box Mode 'a switch to progress'.

It's the mode primarily taught in our education system and used extensively in professions such as engineering, law and finance. One box leads to another, which forms a logical thinking process.

> Let's assume you are thinking of changing where you are renting. What might be some Box Mode questions you could ask yourself?

Box Mode helps you drill down and set yourself (and others) tangible, specific goals.

For example, in Ball Mode you might set yourself a general aim to 'get fit'.

Switch.

In Box Mode you might develop a specific goal of going to the gym three times a week as well as going on a 2-kilometre walk every other day.

The brain science behind Box Mode

Your Box Mode is a metaphor for your central executive network (CEN). Your CEN is like your brain's command centre. It helps you tune out noise—daydreams, doubts, distractions—and zero in on the task. Neuroscientists see it light up during problem-solving, planning or critical thinking.

It's the opposite of mind wandering. Your CEN is deliberate, structured and loves a goal. When CEN is on, the messy stuff fades—you're in the box, so to speak.

When you operate in Box Mode, you use logic, analysis and reason with tools such as the SWOT situation analysis (strengths, weaknesses, opportunities and threats) or the '5 Ws and H' structure used in journalism and business to ensure that every base is covered (what, why, when, who, where and how). AI chatbots such as ChatGPT or Claude are the perfect accelerator of human Box Mode capabilities.

Think small steps rather than big leaps in Box Mode

Box Mode is an efficient way of thinking about situations in a habitual, efficient and safe way. You might think of it as following directions using a LEGO set of bricks to build a model castle.

In many ways, it is the ideal thinking approach for a slow-moving world that values longer-term planning, control, accountability and clearly-defined problems. But this is not the world we face today.

AI in Box Mode

Let's make a leap together. What if AI as well as humans predominantly operate in Box Mode (see figure 2.2)?

Figure 2.2 AI operating in Box Mode

AI was designed by engineers, who primarily think in Box Mode. The emphasis is on efficiency, analysis and accuracy. In Box Mode, AI can summarise large volumes of complex materials at breathtaking speed. It can also evaluate, prioritise and connect your Ball Mode ideas.

This is the only way many people use AI. Yet, as I outline in later chapters, there is also a more creative, expansive way to unleash the full power of this remarkable tool.

The disadvantages of staying in Box Mode

In pressure moments, we often drill down and use the thinking mode we feel most comfortable in. For many of us this is Box Mode. This makes perfect sense as it feels safe, familiar and comfortable.

However, it can cause problems when you face, say, a left-field question in an interview. If you stay in Box Mode, you tend to think narrowly; stick to what you know; follow rules, habits and assumptions; and filter ideas too early.

In Box Mode, you play it safe because you want to avoid embarrassment or making a mistake. So you can hesitate and repeat previous talking points instead of considering that the interviewer might be judging you on your ability to think on the spot.

Being 'stuck in Box Mode' in these moments is an apt description of what happens. You can procrastinate, overthink and become defensive. It is not a question of capability but of rigidity in sticking to the tried and true. You literally get stuck in your own thinking box.

In these circumstances, you need to switch to a different mode of thinking even just for a few minutes.

I call this Ball Mode.

Ball Mode: Switch to possibility

One of my younger daughter's friends asked me for some advice recently about the next step in her career. She asked, 'Do I stay working in my job at the café or go back to university?' I suggested she start to thinking in colours.

'What do you mean?' she said.

'Currently, you're only thinking in black or white. But let's imagine the seven colours in the rainbow (red, orange, yellow, green, blue, indigo and violet)'. Each of these could represent another career possibility. Blue, for example, might represent a blue sky. Perhaps you ought to travel for a year', I suggested.

Her face lit up. Suddenly she saw her situation in a new light: one that was filled with colour, movement and wonder. Perhaps I had helped her switch her thinking from Box Mode to Ball Mode. It certainly felt that way from the energy she was radiating.

Quick quiz: Do you prefer operating in Ball Mode?

For each statement, rate how much you agree:

1 = Strongly disagree

2 = Disagree

3 = Neutral

4 = Agree

5 = Strongly agree

- I enjoy exploring ideas without worrying about practicalities first. ___
- I often make unexpected connections between unrelated things. ___
- I like starting projects even if I don't know exactly how they'll end. ___
- I feel energised when I brainstorm freely without constraints. ___
- I often ask, 'What if…?' or 'Why not…?' to open up new possibilities. ___

If you scored 15 or more, you might prefer operating in Ball Mode—or, at least, that is your preferred starting place.

Let's think about a ball for a moment

Balls are fun, bouncy and energising. You can catch and throw them. You can juggle, hold or squeeze a ball. It's built for movement and imagination. Have a look at the one illustrated in figure 2.3.

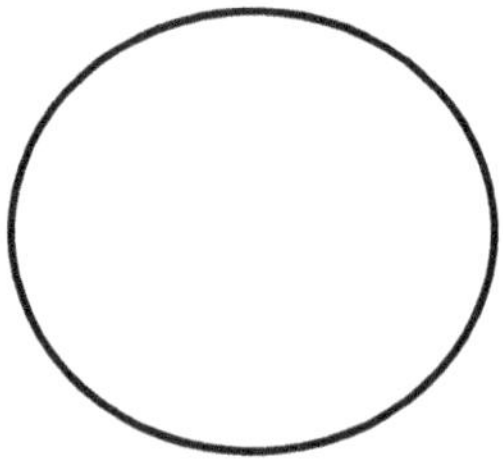

Figure 2.3 Operating in Ball Mode

I always took a ball with me to my workshops and talks over the years.

Why?

Partly because it relaxed me, but it seems to also serve another purpose.

Whenever I showed the participants a ball, I noticed that their body language changed. Their eyes lit up in anticipation; smiles and laughter often ensued. Soon, I started to bring several balls so people could throw them around. I then started to design creative thinking games using the balls.

Switching to Ball Mode

Switching to Ball Mode is often the key to being at your best during any performance situation (e.g. an interview). Box Mode provides you with the preparation, plan and predictability. Switching to Ball Mode gives you the confidence to handle any unexpected or unpredictable moments or make a change because you sense an opportunity. Rather than stay in your familiar Box Mode you switch to Ball Mode, which might lead to a new insight or way of communicating your ideas.

Enter your Default Mode Network (DMN)

Balls come in all sizes and colours. There is no right or wrong ball to use during a workshop and it's something you can use at any age. Just playing with a ball seems to help people return to a more child-like, curious state.

I wondered if this experience triggered something deeper. It seemed to me that participants had switched their thinking before my eyes. This switch is consistent with the latest brain research.

Your DMN is your brain's imaginative, emotional and intuitive side. It's active when you're not focused on the outside world. This network lights up when you daydream, reflect, wander mentally or imagine future possibilities. It can often make remote associations and drive creative thinking even when there is no problem at hand. It can create just because it can!

Your DMN is expansive, imaginative and free flowing. It's what fuels those 'aha' moments that pop up in the shower, on a walk or when you're not trying too hard. This seemed to explain what I had found in my workshops when I encouraged participants to play.

The ball not only became a physical stimulus — for me it became a wonderful new metaphor to use in explaining and communicating the switch from Box Mode to Ball Mode. It was a non-threatening way to present different ways of thinking — such as lateral, creative, systems, associative and visual thinking — in a more accessible way. It meant more people could be more creative and agile, more often!

I found that being in Ball Mode even for a few minutes encouraged people to take more risks and explore change in a more open and playful way — particularly as they knew they could switch back to Box Mode at any time.

It often helped people to make a seemingly small switch in thinking. Yet it also often made a big difference to them, or others, by way of a new insight, solution, question or perspective in real time, whenever they needed it.

The next time you are faced with a challenge, ask yourself 'What won't work?' Then select one of your ideas and in the next 2 minutes try to make it work. What happens?

Move beyond thinking outside the box

Have you ever been asked to think outside the box? It sounds like good advice, but I have found that it's not very helpful.

Why?

First, because most of us don't know how to do it (certainly not on demand).

And second, the moment you say 'think outside the box' you are unconsciously still focusing on the box.

As I just explained, being in Box Mode is a particular style of thinking that is rational, logical and based on previous experiences and patterns. That is why Ball Mode is so exciting. To think outside the box, you need a different mode. A ball is not only a different style, but also a completely different shape.

The situation: Think about a bus that transports people.

Switch: Now think of a bus as a big, moveable advertising billboard.

Another situation: Think of a café as a place to eat.

Switch: You can also think of a café as a place to connect, socialise and work.

The other wonderful advantage of being in Ball Mode or activating your DMN is that your brain is still churning away on your latest problem while you might be having a quick nap, be on a walk or even after a good night's sleep.

John Cleese of *Monty Python* and *Fawlty Towers* fame talks about how he works on new comedy sketches in the evenings. Then, he leaves them and goes to bed not having quite completed them. Miraculously, an ending often emerges in his mind the next morning.

Welcome to the mysterious DMN in action, even when you are not aware of it.

> The next time you (or your team) generate a good idea or solution, take it one step further.
>
> Try making your initial idea nine times better in the next 2 minutes. What emerges will surprise you.

You can use AI in either Box Mode or Ball Mode. All you need are a few simple instructions. These are covered in Appendix B.

AI in Ball Mode

If humans can operate in Ball Mode, why not consider the possibility that AI can also operate in this mode (see figure 2.4)?

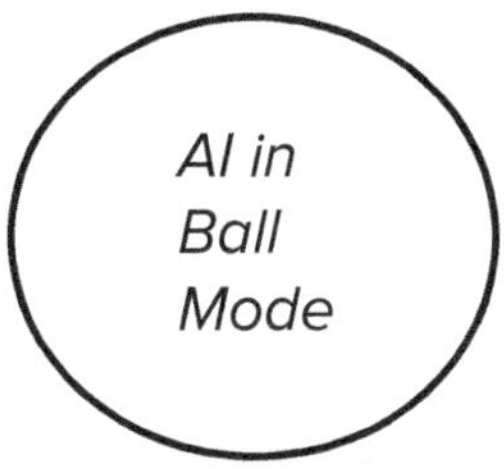

Figure 2.4 Can AI operate in Ball Mode?

It's a very interesting idea.

AI is always available, positive and not threatened by ego concerns or what the boss may be thinking. It can generate numerous ideas, images or videos in no time at all.

It's become one of my creative collaborators and a sounding board. I can be Lennon and AI can be McCartney (or reverse when the need arises). It gives me creative confidence to tackle new problems knowing that it is not judging me.

There are human qualities that AI cannot emulate just yet. Humans can feel, dream and imagine something that has not been developed. You can create meaning and transcend logic with a new story, metaphor, symbol or experience. You can switch! Any yet, even with these limitations, AI often supercharges my initial Ball Mode results.

For example, I often sketch an idea, model or matrix using AI when I wake up in the morning.

My prompt: Perhaps we can invent an eye drop that could help people switch perspectives?

AI's response: Here are three eye-drop categories that you can use:

- Time shift drops to go back or forward in time
- Role switch eye drops (e.g. how might a carpenter see this problem?)
- Fiction eye drops to imagine yourself as a character in a fantasy novel.

What I love about this example is that AI did not say my original idea was silly or cannot be done. It did not let out an audible sigh or cross its arms. AI just went, 'Okay, let's explore it'.

The disadvantages of staying in Ball Mode

As much as I love being in Ball Mode, it does have some disadvantages. When you are facing a moment that matters, you can fall in love with your own ideas (or those of others) and ignore or downplay the practical and commercial feasibility of them.

In Ball Mode you are interested primarily in novel ideas or solutions rather than implementation. This can be exciting and energising but without an action this remains potential, not performance.

You can become overwhelmed with numerous ideas in Ball Mode. Rather than evaluating and prioritising your existing ideas, you are attracted to the next big, shiny toy. Think of a juggler with too many balls in the air — eventually one will drop.

My younger daughter tells me this all the time. Because of her ADHD she sometimes feels overwhelmed with new stimuli and ideas. So, the issue for her is not creating new possibilities but deciding which ones to move forward on. Her challenge is planning, prioritising and getting started. Switching to Box Mode deliberately is perfect for her.

It's why I have suggested to her that she should use a '10 to 2 formula' at work. Spend 10 minutes in Box Mode then 2 minutes in Ball Mode creating and imagining. This acknowledges and gives her permission to play with new possibilities while the bulk of her time is spent achieving her goals.

Being in Ball Mode can also mean that you ruminate more than you need to. Switching to Box Mode can help you deal with 'what is' rather than 'what if' or 'what could be'. To extend the ball metaphor: sometimes balls are heavy. Think of a bowling ball, for example, or a medicine ball at the gym. Ruminating on a potential mistake can feel very heavy.

Ball Mode ideas can often be far removed from reality, capability or available resources. This means they are more like balloons that you glimpse for a while, then in a strong wind they float away. This can involve greater risk, uncertainty and unpredictability (although there is always the risk of doing nothing).

Think Box Mode and Ball Mode

To date I have described the two modes in Switch Thinking: Box Mode and Ball Mode. You might be forgiven for thinking that these are two quite different modes of thinking because you are correct. But it is not a case of one versus the other as some people have suggested with, say, critical thinking or creative thinking.

Think of Box Mode *and* Ball Mode.

These are just two sides of the same coin. You need both and you can switch between modes depending on the moment.

This switching, connecting and interacting leads to a bigger idea. When you do this, you actually multiply your ideas, solutions and insights. When structure and imagination interact, for example, the impact is multiplied. You can create breakthrough ideas that work.

That's why it's more accurate to think in terms of Box Mode × Ball Mode. In fact, recent neuroscience research shows that creativity depends not on being imaginative or analytical, but on the ability to dynamically switch between brain networks. In the research, creative individuals could use their DMN to generate ideas, then switch to their CEN to evaluate and refine these.

But here is the kicker.

The more they switched between the two networks using their salience network, the more creative they were. Switching between the different networks was the magic sauce.

It's why I call it Box Mode × Ball Mode.

The full potential of these modes is using them in combination. Much like mixed martial artists, who have learned that a punch, followed by a kick, then, say, an arm bar hold, is a more dynamic and powerful combination than, say, a single punch.

Here is another example. Our values and purpose are created in Ball Mode. These emerge from asking ourselves such questions as 'What matters to me?' 'What do I care about?' and 'How can I contribute?' These are invaluable starting points but these need to be shaped, defined and communicated in Box Mode.

There is no right or wrong mode to operate in. The key message is that you can operate in either mode depending on the situation or moment, then switch to the other mode for a few minutes to see what emerges. Much like learning how to play the piano, the left hand is used for structure, rhythm and grounding, and the right hand is for melody, expression and variation. Yet beautiful music is composed when both hands play together: they are in sync, not one hand dominating over the other.

As I have mentioned, many people struggle because they stick to a single mode at the exact time when they should be switching. It's the switching and connecting between the two modes that can help you be at your best when it really matters.

In later chapters I will describe how you can easily make the switch between different modes using any of the 6 switches for a 2-minute time frame. This is key. I have found that even under pressure you can switch to a new mode for a few minutes. You can try something new at the same time as feeling safe if it is done quickly. And you can always switch back. It's like switching gears on a bike: you are in control as you switch gears to meet the contours and difficulty of the road in front of you. A small switch, when you need it, can make all the difference.

Switch Thinking and *The Pitt*

Have you seen the award-winning medical TV series *The Pitt*? It's set in the emergency department of a large hospital in the United States. Each episode unfolds in near real time, following a team of doctors and nurses across a single, relentless 15-hour shift. The appeal of the program is the diverse characters, the relationships between the staff and the patients, and the medicine itself. With real doctors as part of the writing team, the operating procedures are both spellbinding and very graphic.

This show reminds me so much of Switch Thinking in action. There are patients who need help in a hurry; emotions are high and outcomes are uncertain. These are real moments that matter.

Depending on the situation, most of the doctors start in Box Mode. They require certain information quickly (e.g. blood pressure readings); there are protocols, and checklists with clear roles and chains of command. The attending doctors methodically assess the patient and decide on a course of action.

And yet…

There are situations that don't go as planned. A patient doesn't present according to the textbook, beds are not available or the patient's vitals start to go south.

In these moments, the doctors pause and switch to Ball Mode: a more open, adaptive, creative way of thinking. They improvise. They draw on experience, intuition and empathy. They see the situation from a different angle or reframe what really matters right now.

This is often where the most human moments occur: calming a terrified patient, navigating a family conflict or finding an unconventional solution when the obvious options are gone.

And then, when the patient (hopefully) is stable, the doctor and the team switch back to Box Mode. This is the core insight: performance during moments that matter isn't about staying in one mode — it's about matching the mode to the moment. To use a left-field example, think of how an octopus can change colours to blend in with its environment to escape a predator.

Being able to switch from one mode of thinking to another is not just limited to the emergency room. You can learn to do this anywhere, anytime, by yourself or with others. This is the real magic, to me, of a show such as *The Pitt*. You can see how individuals and a team switch; how they think, feel and act in real time to be in sync with the moment and each other.

2-minute Switch Thinking exercise

I was recently on a trek in the middle of Australia and enjoying every moment of this vast landscape. My mind was wandering, and I saw a flock of birds. I said to the person I was walking with, 'Imagine if you were a bird and you feared heights'.

This caused some amusement and led to a fun discussion of what other animals might suffer from a similar challenge (e.g. imagine a snake that was scared of the dark).

This is switching at its most innocent. You are activating your Ball Mode (i.e. DMN) just for fun. Now imagine being able to do this on demand! It could be on a walk, in the shower or when you are doodling.

Imagine being able to also engage your team's collective DMN by helping them switch to Ball Mode.

Here's how.

When you or others are stuck, you simply say, 'Why don't we try a switch in thinking for the next 2 minutes? For example, let's switch the goal. What might be a surprising goal that would energise the group? What is a goal that we would love to work towards?'

See what emerges.

You can always switch back to the original goal.

Chapter 3

Switch and connect

Imagine you are at the theatre watching a play and you are right up the front. You can see the actors' facial expressions and every tiny movement. You are focused on the details (i.e. a Box Mode lens).

At interval, however, you move to a seat on the top floor (with permission of course). Now you can see the entire stage and appreciate the cleverness of how the set has been designed. You have switched to a broader view of the situation. The actors, set and costumes have not changed, but from this higher seat the performance looks slightly different (i.e. a Ball Mode lens). You can then switch back to your original seat if you wish.

This oscillation, depending on the moment, is Switch Thinking in operation. See figure 3.1 for a graphic representation.

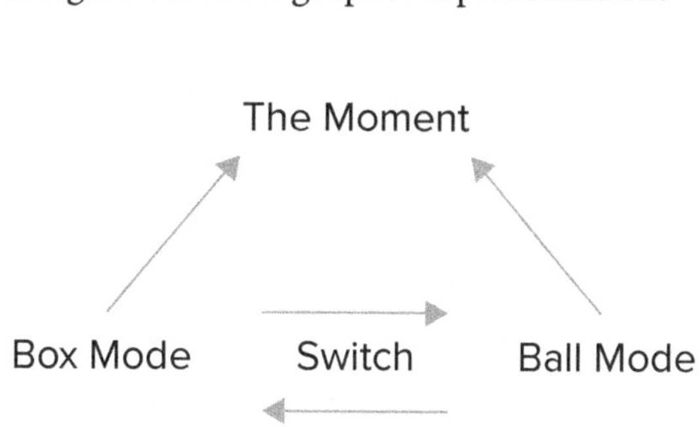

Figure 3.1 Switch Thinking in operation

Switch Thinking gives you the tools to make a change in how you think at any moment — on demand. You pause, switch and play to either create a new possibility (i.e. Ball Mode) or make progress (i.e. Box Mode).

The situation: Think about a car as an internal combustion engine.

Switch: Think about a car as a big computer on wheels.

Which of these ways of thinking is more future based?

Another way to change your thinking is to change the situation or physical location (if you can). It's why travelling to another country can be so invigorating. You are faced with a world that might be quite different from what you are used to. On a much smaller scale, you can go for a walk or meet someone for a coffee at a new café. Anything to break free of your usual thinking.

The problem with this approach, however, is that you might not always be able to change your physical environment when you want to, but a different way of thinking is always accessible.

The situation: You think of people riding electric bikes as a pain when you are driving.

Switch: You can also think that electric bikes are a way to encourage more people to exercise, reduce car traffic and they are better for the environment than driving.

Switch Thinking as I have described it is the process of switching back and forth between Box Mode and Ball Mode (for accuracy please note that Box Mode and Ball Mode are metaphors for patterns of brain network activity, not literal on/off states). The magic I have found is not only in the switch but in the interaction between the two. Think of a car that has an accelerator and a brake — you need both to drive.

Tools like the 2-minute switch, switch off & switch on and the 6 switches (the latter is covered in chapters 7 to 12) provide the mechanism to switch between these two modes.

Switching between Box Mode and Ball Mode

There is nothing inherently right or wrong about either Box Mode or Ball Mode. They are equally valuable. The goal is to sync each mode to a moment that matters (e.g. if you are brainstorming you might start in Ball Mode and if you are talking to your tax agent you might commence in Box Mode).

But note that these are starting modes. You can change. You can switch between the two modes whenever you wish. The only time an issue might arise is when you stay too long in one mode or use a mode that does not suit the moment. The true potential of Box Mode and Ball Mode is when you use them together.

You pause for a moment, consider the moment, then switch and play for a few minutes. Refer to figure 3.2 to see this in action.

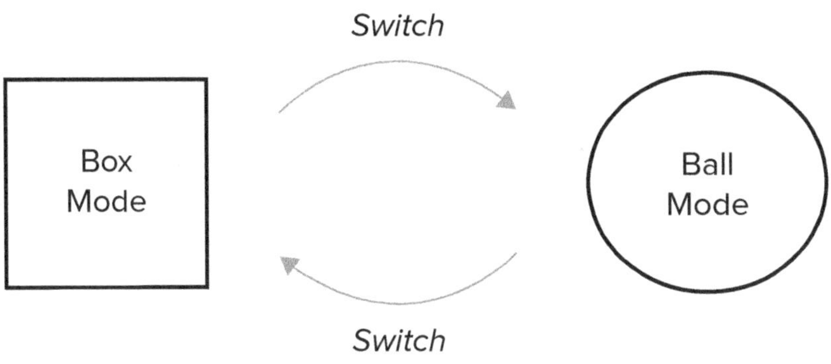

Figure 3.2 **Switching from Box Mode to Ball Mode**

The key point about figure 3.2 is that the switch goes both ways. You can switch from a more structured thinking approach (i.e. Box Mode) to a more unstructured mode (i.e. Ball Mode) and you can switch back again. You control which mode you wish to think in and for how long. It's like switching between talking and listening. Both are needed to have a meaningful conversation.

The situation: In Box Mode you might ask, 'How can I improve the customer experience by 1 per cent?'

Switch: In Ball Mode you might ask, 'What could transform the customer experience by 100 per cent?'

Both questions are valid. They are just different; the former can help you and your clients right now. And a series of smaller 1 per cent improvements add up. A 100 per cent transformation might give you a bigger, longer term advantage.

You have more influence over your mode of thinking than you realise. And this insight is, for many people, a real 'aha' moment.

This is the core idea of Switch Thinking. A switch, as the name implies, is a deliberate attempt to create or swap to a different thinking mode. It's what your brain's salience network is doing automatically.

Think of each mode as being available to you (and others) and at any time you can minimise or enlarge them. You decide which mode is in the foreground and which is in the background (see figure 3.3).

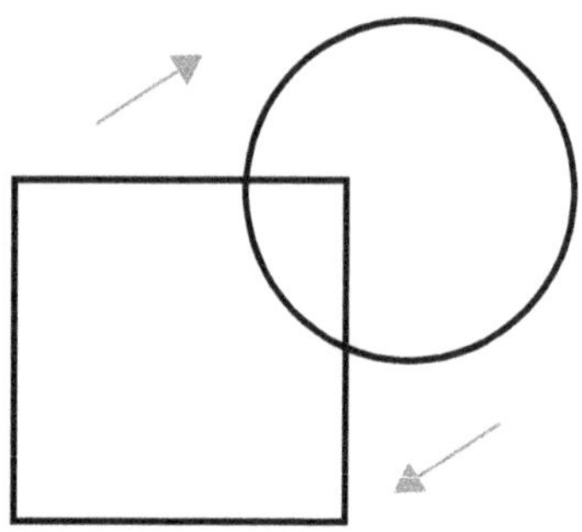

Figure 3.3 What's your starting mode?

Recent brain research suggests that the more frequently you switch from Box Mode to Ball Mode (i.e. CEN to DMN), the higher the creativity. This research challenges one of the principles of brainstorming, whereby evaluation is held at the end of a session. A more effective approach is to continually create using Ball Mode, then switch to Box Mode to evaluate.

To date I have been talking about switching between Box Mode and Ball Mode. But this idea can be extended to also mean switching between humans and AI; and between individuals and a group. This takes the idea of switching to another, higher level of collaboration, creativity and adaptation.

Switching between humans and AI

In chapter 2 (Box Mode × Ball Mode) I suggested that Box Mode includes both humans and AI. Operating in Ball Mode could also include humans and AI.

This means you could have four collaborative possibilities, as presented in figure 3.4 (overleaf):

- *Structured collaboration*
  In this case, both humans and AI are in Box Mode. This switching back and forth is ideal for analysis, testing and planning where the emphasis is on speed and accuracy.
- *Creative efficiency*
  In this quadrant, humans are in Box Mode and AI is in Ball Mode. Your AI is prompted to generate ideas to a challenge, then you switch back to human evaluation and judgement. It's creativity within limits.
- *Guided discovery*
  In this quadrant, humans are in Ball Mode, using prompts such as 'What if?' and AI provides Box Mode real-world feedback and evaluation. This means that imaginative leaps are still anchored in probability.

- *Total creativity*
  This is where both humans and AI have switched to Ball Mode. Both AI and humans are sparking off one another, pushing the limits of imagination and possibility.

  This quadrant can be very powerful because human creativity can be multiplied by AI creativity. It's not 4 units of human creativity added to 4 units of AI creativity (equals 8); instead, it's 4 units *times* another 4 units (equals 16).

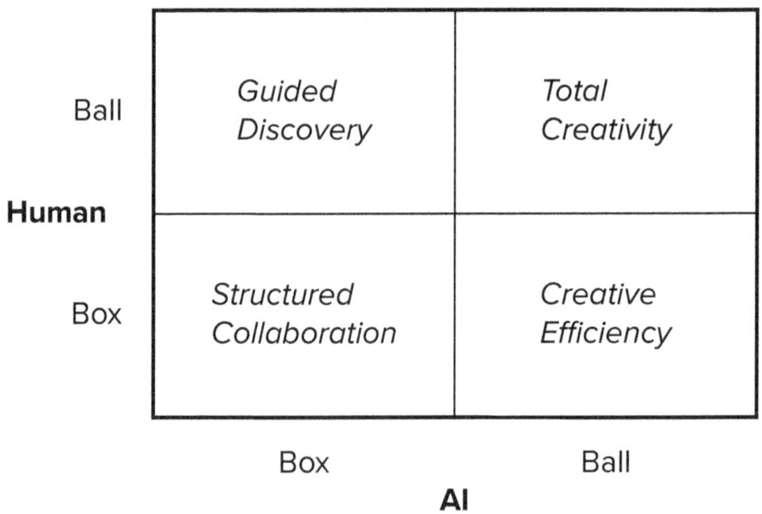

Figure 3.4 Human and AI interactions

Total creativity, I believe, is the future of human and AI innovation and growth. Think of a multiplier effect, rather than defending creativity as being only a human capability. Have you ever seen dolphins or orcas playing and hunting? Creativity surely is spread far and wide. Perhaps the idea of AI creativity does not seem such a stretch. This idea is explored more fully in chapter 6 (Prompt imagining).

I find switching between human and AI Box and Ball Modes incredibly exciting. This type of collaboration and interaction is far more nuanced and varied than the one-way approach most of us currently use (i.e. human in Box Mode, AI in Box Mode). This 4-quadrant approach offers far more potential for breakthroughs in a shorter time.

Another model of human and technological co-creating is CGI — which stands for computer-generated imagery — is used in films. Think of *Avatar*, *Jurassic Park* and the *Terminator* series as well as other films that have woven human imagination with the latest technology to create memorable moments. This fusion is a guide to future individual and collective human and AI interactions.

Switching between the individual and the group

There is nothing better than working with someone who is on the same page as you. In the world of Switch Thinking, this often means you are both in either Box Mode or Ball Mode.

When you are both in Box Mode you are focused on a goal, aware of what resources are available and what you must deliver and when. In Ball Mode you are both sparking off each other as you build on each other's ideas. This can be fun and energising.

However, problems can arise if you are each using a different mode at the same time. One of you might be trying to open the discussion, while the other is trying to focus it. Or someone is trying to plan the next steps, and the other person is floating another left-field idea.

To avoid this situation, pause and simply ask your thinking partner or the group:

What mode are you in now?
What mode do we need to be in at this moment?

These simple questions can ensure that everyone is in sync. And remember, the mode you agree to start in may not be the mode you end up in. You can change!

Connecting

Let's upgrade the model of Switch Thinking—see figure 3.5.

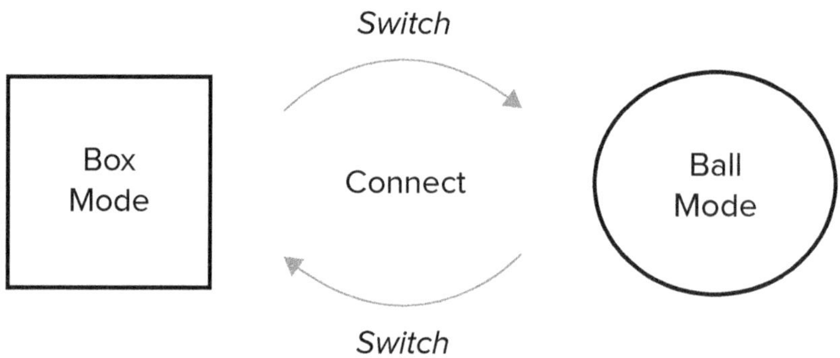

Figure 3.5 **The Switch Thinking Connect model**

Rather than just switching back and forth, you can also try to connect the ideas, suggestions or images that emerge from Box Mode and Ball Mode.

Connecting is often an overlooked step in any creative, innovative or problem-solving process. In this voluntary step, you are proactively searching for ways to make a bigger and better solution.

For example, you can start in Box Mode, define the problem and develop a few initial ideas, then switch to Ball Mode to generate a few more original ideas. Then try to connect the safe with the more adventurous ideas and see what emerges.

Or you could start in Ball Mode with perhaps a big long-term goal. Then switch to Box Mode for a tangible few steps to start working on today. Then try to connect the two. What emerges?

I call this connecting step my 'fruit salad approach'. If you have a banana, an apple, an orange and a strawberry, these are all fine to eat by themselves. But if you combine these and add some yogurt you have fruit salad — a more comprehensive eating option.

AI is wonderful at making random connections. It's not wedded to a particular mindset or worried that connecting an idea might lead to a ridiculous outcome. After you have developed some ideas in Box Mode, switch to Ball Mode and develop a few more. Then ask AI to try to connect these. I have often been surprised at what happens.

You can connect using Box Mode or Ball Mode. In Box Mode you might connect based on function, process or need. It could be that you try to connect a customer need with a new product. This is a practical, grounded and often linear approach.

In Ball Mode you are looking for more lateral, playful and imaginative connections. For example, an emergency care doctor I spoke to recently indicated that she still connects with the skills she learned when working in retail (while at university) to deal with sometimes stressed, angry customers.

The connecting key: Think 'and', not 'or'

The idea of thinking 'and', not 'or' is a switch in itself.

It's moving beyond compromise to connection. When you compromise, you accept that to reach agreement every party must give up something. When you connect, on the other hand, it encourages you to search for a third way. One that builds on the ideas in both modes 'and' transforms these into something else. Consider Paralympics as an example. This wonderful concept connects world-class athletes with the Olympic Games to celebrate what is possible in human achievement.

The idea of emergence

You can push the idea of connecting even further, as illustrated in figure 3.6. Sometimes when you connect two quite different ideas, you create something quite new. Think of 'brunch': it's a combination of breakfast and lunch, yet it's something quite different. Or have you tried pickleball? It's one of the fastest growing sports in the world. It's like tennis, badminton and table tennis, yet it has its own character, rules and equipment.

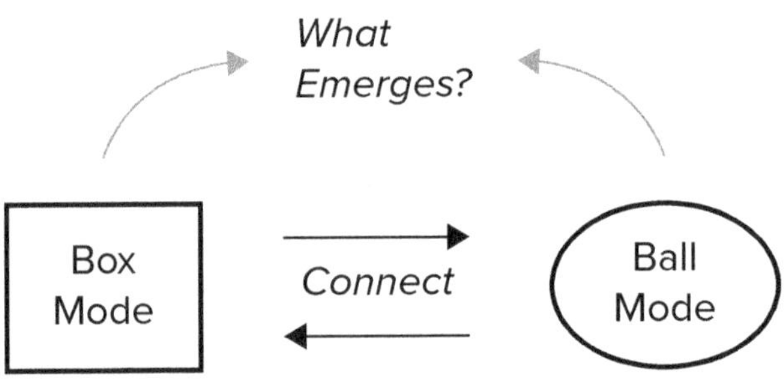

Figure 3.6 A Switch Thinking model of emergence

In short, a new sport (e.g. pickleball) has emerged from connecting elements of other sports. And often, out of these connections there is an emergent idea, insight or solution. It can happen in a conversation, at a dinner party or during any interaction where there is openness, flexibility and some structure.

Connecting and emergence

One of my favourite TV series is the UK's *Portrait Artist of the Year.* Anyone can send in a self-portrait, which is evaluated by a judging panel. Each episode consists of nine artists (professional and amateur) who have been selected from their entries and each is given the challenge of painting three guest celebrities in the space of 4 hours. Then a winner is selected to proceed to a semi-final and perhaps to a final.

What I love about this program is the variety of artists, styles, techniques, materials and guests. The program itself is creative, encouraging and optimistic. Some artists start in what I have described as Box Mode. The emphasis is on accurate proportions, framing and composition. Then they switch to a more interpretive expression. They let go of the safety of structure and take more risks with colour as they attempt to capture the sitter's character, mood and energy.

Other artists start in a completely different way. They use broad brush strokes, work quickly and want to capture first impressions and raw emotions. Then they switch back to Box Mode to check such things as accuracy, likeness and composition.

Over the 4 hour-period, you see the painters — regardless of which mode they started in — regularly switch between the two modes. If they are happy with their progress they might step back for a few minutes, reconsider, perhaps study the sitter for a few moments and press on (Box Mode). If they are stuck, they might consider a completely different colour or background (Ball Mode). They alternate between careful rendering and broad strokes, often in a moment.

What is also interesting for me is that they use language like 'I had a bit of a plan but the painting sort of emerged in front of me' or 'I surprised myself with how the painting ended up'. This is emergence happening in the switch between different modes of thinking, feeling and, in this case, painting.

This is a common feeling among people in my workshops when they are using Switch Thinking. They are frequently surprised at what they create, connect and learn in moments that matter.

2-minute Switch Thinking exercise

The usual way to solve a problem or overcome a barrier is to start with your current solution and move forward.

In the next 2 minutes, try switching to the perfect or ideal solution.

What does it look like? Forget any restrictions such as timing, skills or budget.

My perfect solution or result is...

Now start building a step-by-step approach to move towards your perfect solution or result.

Chapter 4

The 2-minute switch

If you have ever watched a football (i.e. soccer) game when Lionel Messi is playing you might have wondered what all the fuss is about. He seems to wander around the field for ages, then in a split second he does something wondrous — it might be a defence-splitting pass or a match-winning goal.

There are great players, and then there is Messi.

In a time-poor world, where attention spans are short and you are under pressure to deliver results, a few minutes can matter.

This is why Switch Thinking is built around 2-minute bursts. It can help you during those important moments and often it is all you need to get unstuck and open your mind to new possibilities.

There is also another reason why 2 minutes can be your secret weapon. This short time frame is like a shot of caffeine in the morning: it accelerates your thinking and unleashes amazing energy and creativity. I call this Speed Thinking and it is based on a fascinating insight.

Speed Thinking

A few years ago, I developed a concept called Speed Thinking and wrote a book by the same name.

Speed Thinking was built on watching leaders work in groups for an hour on a challenge (e.g. how to increase revenue by 20 per cent in 3 years). I noticed that while there was lots of talking, not much happened until I opened the door and said '10 minutes to go'. Then there was a sudden burst of energy and often the group came up with some wonderful ideas — seemingly out of nowhere.

I became interested in what happened in that 10 minutes. There was a deadline — urgency — and respondents could not procrastinate or rely only on rigorous analysis. They had to create something — in a hurry! They had no time to second guess themselves or to filter their responses. As such, they were free to create.

Think of improv actors and jazz musicians. They don't wait for ideas — they act. They trust their Ball Mode (i.e. DMN) to generate surprising moves and notes.

Thinking at a rapid pace helps you quieten your inner critic and unlock your creativity — so much so, in fact, that people in my workshops would often say things like:

'I didn't know I could think like that!'

'That idea just appeared!'

'It felt fun — like a creative burst'.

When I was developing Speed Thinking I played with various accelerated time periods. I had the most success when I suggested to people that they had only 2 minutes to start solving a problem. Leaders surprised themselves at what they could come up with in 2 minutes. I called this process Speed Thinking. It has led me to what I now call 'the 2-minute switch'.

In many situations, to change how you think, feel and act you may only have to switch for 2 minutes at a time. In 2 minutes, you can create a new idea, gain a fresh insight or ask a new question in a meeting.

Or change your thinking mode and see what happens. Switch Thinking is a wonderful combination of creative thinking and speed thinking. You can change direction @ speed!

And just like Speed Thinking, the 2-minute switch is fun, energising, creative and efficient. Think of it as a mental sprint, not a jog.

My 2-minute workout

Every hour when I am working at my computer I try to do a 2-minute workout. It consists of 20 push-ups, 100 punches on my punching bag outside my office and a 1-minute jog on my adult trampoline. It's a tiny workout, I know. But I always feel good after it. Whatever I was worried about before the workout tends to slip away—or at least I think about it in a more imaginative way.

In just 2 minutes of activity, I act (heart rate increases), feel (more energised) and think differently (often leads to a breakthrough).

This has the added benefit that, over the course of a day and over a few months, my fitness level has increased. Now, I am not suggesting that you must smash a punching bag. You could just go for a walk, work on something else or make yourself a cup of tea. The 2-minute switch is both a means to an end (i.e. to switch how you think, feel and act) and an end in itself (i.e. a simple, accessible way to lead a healthier life).

The other lesson from my 2-minute physical workout is that I decide when to do it. I do not have to wait for the right time, people or location. I just get going. If I can do this with physical activity, why not with my thinking? Why wait for the right time, place or mood to try switching your thinking?

This insight is both empowering and exciting. You are free to switch anywhere, anytime, with anyone.

For the next 2 minutes, imagine yourself on holidays. What are you doing, feeling and looking forward to? Can you hear the laughter of your friends or family? Use this feeling while working on whatever problem is in front of you right now.

Switch and play for 2 minutes

Based on what I have experienced in my workshops, and personal experience, I have found that 2 minutes is the ideal time frame for switching your thinking. It has become the core of my switch-thinking approach. It's why I suggest that you can change your life, one small switch at a time.

The 2-minute time frame is also ideal for the 'during' phase of any performance cycle, as illustrated in figure 4.1.

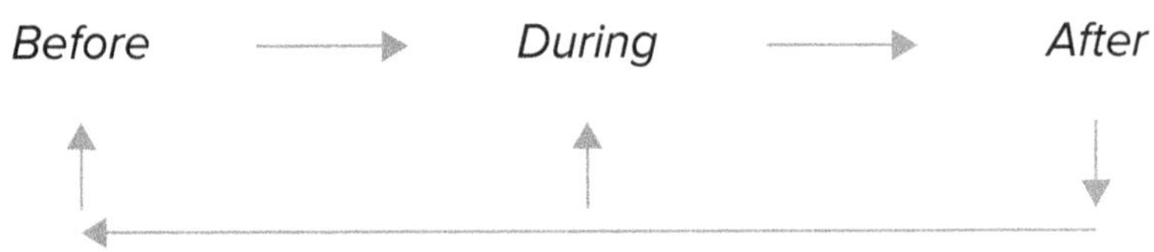

Figure 4.1 Switch Thinking in the moment

This is the neglected area of performance, coaching and leading. Switch Thinking gives you the tools to play the game better while you are in the middle of the match. It's not the warm-up or half-time pep talk. Nor is it the post-match talk. It empowers you during a presentation, sales call, exam, conversation with your partner or kids, or during a team meeting.

It gives you a way to switch your thinking from your default to a different approach when you need it. Not before or after, but during.

What's more, I have found that even the most rigid, rules-bound person can accept the logic of switching for just 2 minutes. I ask them, 'Why don't you switch to Ball Mode for just 2 minutes and start playing with whatever switch you selected?' When they do, they often surprise themselves with the new ideas or possibilities that emerge.

And this is the key. You play with ideas, suggestions and raw thoughts without evaluation. You are in a sandpit in your mind as your imagination is given free rein. For many people this is incredibly liberating. They give themselves and others 2 minutes of mental play time.

'You can go back to your usual way at any time', I suggest. This is key. I have found that you are often more willing to take a risk if it's only for 2 minutes. It's a bit like trying an appetiser rather than risking the main meal on something that you may not like.

The situation: How am I planning to spend this weekend?

Switch for 2 minutes: What are nine things I have never done on a weekend?

Paragliding, you might say. Why not give it a go?

The 2-minute switch is short, fun and energising. Think of it as a micro-shift with macro potential. The sprint means you can rush by all the barriers that often slow you down or hold you back (e.g. I could never do that; I am not good enough). And after your cognitive sprint you can always switch back to a slower, more sustainable pace.

The 2 minutes is not just about thinking at an accelerated pace but also switching to something new.

You can switch to a new perspective, focus, assumption or question.

The situation: What's a win for me in this situation?

Switch for 2 minutes: What's a win for my partner, neighbourhood or community? (Remember: don't filter.)

What emerged? How did it feel?

By switching to a new mode, you might generate a fresh insight or possibility, and the compressed time limit gives you the safety to try. Just go for it!

That 'aha' moment

On a trip to England with one of my New Zealand friends, Paul, he suggested we go and watch the cricket at Lords. I jumped at the chance.

Paul had recently purchased two pubs, one of which was making money; the other not so much. I asked him why. He replied, 'Alcohol margins are small, times are tough and many patrons have got out of the habit of going to the pub'.

I asked him, 'What do you see when you think about your pub?'

'A place for drinking', he offered.

'In 2 minutes', I said, 'tell me what else it could be'.

He instantly started thinking of a space for socialising, fun, advice and connecting. He soon had an 'aha' moment: 'I am going to transform the top half of the pub into 10-room accommodation'. Paul quickly went to work, employed an architect, engaged a builder and with some local government support he was off and running.

When I saw him 12 months later, he said, 'Thank you. My revenue has doubled, and I am finally making a profit. The future looks very promising'.

This is a story about Paul's openness to change, a willingness to try something new and an expanded way of thinking. A simple switch in less than 2 minutes made a big difference.

The empowering aspect of this idea is in exploring a different possibility for a short time rather than relying on your automatic first response. In the workplace, this might look like this:

The situation: You need to have a tough conversation with a colleague about their performance.

You pause: Which mode should I start in?

- Box Mode: Start with all the areas in which they have fallen short.
- Ball Mode: Start with asking about their life. What is happening? Be open, listen, ask questions.

By starting in Ball Mode, you might just have opened the door to a better outcome.

You can switch in either direction: from Box Mode to Ball Mode or the reverse. This means you have greater flexibility and agility in how you respond to any situation.

You do not have to continue with what you have always thought, felt or done.

As one of my participants in a Switch Thinking workshop observed when I introduced the 2-minute switch to the group: 'I love this, Ken, and it's such a practical gateway to unlocking creativity. Most people wait to feel inspired before they act, but the 2-minute sprint flips that. You act, and inspiration follows. The magic happens when we trade control for curiosity'.

The 2-minute switch is the ideal way of *not* being locked into a fixed mindset. You are building a more creative, agile thinking habit. Much like getting up from your desk every hour to stretch; or perhaps saying hello to someone new at your local café (I know this is scary). It's both continuity and interruption.

Situation: I need to make a decision about my career.

Pause: What's my usual way of making a decision? Who do I talk to?

Switch: What decision might an entrepreneur come to?

Play: Explore the more entrepreneurial option. What emerges?

The 2-minute time frame is perfect for AI

In fact, it's probably 1 minute, 45 seconds too long!

In the next 2 minutes, using AI, you can ask:

- a 'what if' type question (e.g. 'What if you could rent a robot for a day or a week. What would it do?')
- how to develop a launch plan for a new business idea you might have
- how to make a new, left-field career move
- what are five new holiday ideas you have never considered.

This turns the 2-minute switch into a human and AI creative and collaborative loop. You bring the curiosity and imagination; AI brings the speed and processing power.

The 2-minute switch is also ideal for groups and teams

Do you want to release some energy into a meeting or brainstorming session? Here's a suggestion.

Make sure that everyone in the team understands the challenge.

Next, ask everyone to work by themselves for 2 minutes trying to generate as many ideas as they can.

Then, ask them to work in pairs for a few minutes discussing each other's initial ideas. The emphasis should be on speed and building on each other's ideas.

In a short while you will have the entire group buzzing with energy and ideas. Have each pairing then present their best ideas to another pairing, then eventually to the bigger group.

I have found that if you want the group to be creative, start with the individual. And that dynamic starts with a 2-minute sprint.

Set yourself a 2-minute switch goal

I try to practise and develop my switch-thinking muscle every day. My goal is to become better at switching so it simply becomes the way I create, solve and decide.

Start by trying to use the word 'switch' at least once per day. It could be with someone else or just to yourself. You could be working on a problem, how you are feeling or what you are doing.

Here's an example.

The situation: Perhaps you might be feeling overwhelmed with a new project you have been given.

Switch for 2 minutes: What are three concrete steps you can make today to kick off the new project?

I have found that just using the word 'switch' a few times around others often results in them adopting the word (even unconsciously).

I recently attended a skin specialist for a checkup, and I found his manner quite sharp. Rather than getting upset, I tried to see the situation from his perspective. I quickly realised that he was running late and perhaps felt bad that he was behind in his appointments. Did this switch in perspective help me? Absolutely — although I am reconsidering whether I will go back to see him again — but at least his frustration did not jump over to me.

Microlearning and the 2-minute switch

One of the more recent trends in learning and development is the idea of microlearning. As the name suggests, this is where there is a short, intensive and bite-size learning experience.

This approach has a number of advantages, including:

- learners are only having to deal with one idea, not a complex set of materials.
- it is often more interactive, time efficient and works well with a decreasing attention span.

The results are impressive, with greater comprehension, engagement, completion rates, skill acquisition and desired behavioural changes.

The 2-minute switch, I believe, is a powerful example of this microlearning approach. There's typically a focus on one switch, the time invested is short (i.e. 2 minutes), it is experiential (i.e. involves a switch in thinking) and the results are immediate. It is also modular because you can use one switch, then move to another.

Microlearning is, it seems, here to stay. Switch Thinking in 2-minute bursts is the ideal way to learn, practise and develop this life skill.

Blitz chess as an example of 2-minute switching

Have you ever watched blitz chess being played? It's a blur of moves and counter moves. Each player has 10 minutes or less to make all their moves. It is fast, energising and players often rely more on intuition and pattern recognition than detailed analysis. The board and the pieces are the same but it is played at a lightning pace.

Blitz chess is fast, no question about it, but it also calls for a different way of thinking and playing the game. You cannot calculate every move, nor wait for certainty. So you must think faster and differently, just like a 2-minute switch.

Players can still use Box Mode to have a rough starting plan, defend when required and make quick evaluations. But they also have to switch to Ball Mode and use their intuition, and to make surprising moves and even creative sacrifices. The key is to switch back and forth between Box Mode and Ball Mode depending on the moment, opposition and state of the game. Players switch from, say, calculating to feeling; from control to letting go.

The 2-minute switch works in the same way. It frees you up to move forward, stop over-analysing and create a new possibility. You create, imagine and decide, all in a few minutes.

What blitz has done to classical chess, Switch Thinking offers as a needed alternative to traditional thinking. It is an adaptation of the old model of long-term planning, control, and rational, logical decision making. This old-model world does not exist anymore. The goal is not to slow you down but to help you think differently at speed, when you need to.

The 2-minute aspect of Switch Thinking helps you switch to a different brain network. It can lead to an emergence of new ideas, fits with how people work and live, and works beautifully with the speed of AI.

This is not to say the old approach to chess or thinking is wrong. It's just that you have a choice. You get to decide how you want to think, feel and act, when you need to, on your terms.

2-minute Switch Thinking exercise

Have a few 'go-to' switches and prompts on hand.

Imagine being able to switch on your imagination whenever you need to. To do this, I often use:

- I wonder...
- What if?
- What does the perfect or ideal solution look like?

I use these when I am working on a challenge, with another person or with AI. Having a few prompts up your sleeve takes the pressure off and you can make a start and gain momentum.

In my workshops over the years, to start things off I often suggest how a clown might view a problem or situation. Clowns are fun, playful and colourful. And I know this switch works. People instantly start talking about magic, surprise, big noses, and so on. They have switched their thinking without even noticing it.

Chapter 5

Switch off and switch on

My wife loves 'to-do' lists. They give her life order and structure, and help her prioritise what is important. This approach makes perfect sense. It's logical, linear and most importantly it works for her. It's the most efficient way she has found to achieve her goals for the day, week and month.

In short, 'to-do' lists help her get from point A to B (see figure 5.1) with minimal effort and maximum results.

Figure 5.1 **Getting from point A to point B**

To-do lists are a classic example of Box Mode thinking in action. They are simple, useful and practical. As we have seen, much of our thinking day to day is in Box Mode. These default thinking patterns become habits, processes, scripts and ways of thinking, feeling and acting that are familiar, predictable and conserve energy.

However, there are situations or moments when relying on Box Mode does not work. It could when your budget is cut in half, someone important in your team has just resigned or a deadline has been brought forward. In these moments there is a barrier and there is no clear-cut path to achieve your (or the team's) goals, meaning progress is stalled (see figure 5.2, overleaf).

Figure 5.2 Progress is stalled

In these circumstances you cannot keep thinking, feeling and acting in the same way without running into the same barrier. This moment calls for a new response. You must change, adapt or react in a different way (see figure 5.3).

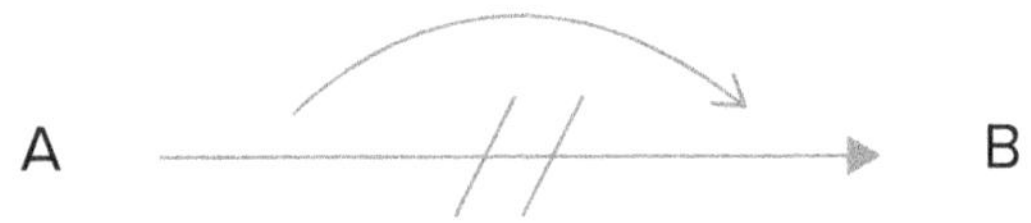

Figure 5.3 You need to switch

This means going around the barrier to reach your goal (i.e. point B). The goal is not to keep bashing your head against the wall hoping the situation will change. In short, you need to switch to Ball Mode thinking. This might mean switching such things as your focus, perspective and questions.

What I like about this approach is that you have not abandoned your usual, efficient way of thinking (i.e. Box Mode). You realise that there are many ways to reach your goal and when your first approach does not work there is always another way. This means you need to go around, over or under the barrier and resume your path.

Notice too how Box Mode and Ball Mode work together. It's not one or the other—both are needed at different times, much like the striker in football needs the midfielder and defender to work hard, tackle and win the ball, and deliver the ball to the striker to hopefully score the goal. The striker might receive the glory but only because of the efforts of their teammates. This applies to thinking as well.

Ball Mode feels exciting, but it works only when it is supported by the discipline of Box Mode thinking.

An instant switch

One way of switching between Box Mode and Ball Mode is what I call 'switch off and switch on'. As the name implies, you try to 'switch off' Box Mode and 'switch on' Ball Mode for 2 minutes, much like you might switch to a different channel on your TV. It's a small, safe and exploratory act that can help you discover new solutions and possibilities. Think small switches with instant impact.

Much like professional tennis players, who switch off in between games to reset and relax, it's a quick, simple and dynamic way to change the channels in your mind from one you always use to a different one. I think the genius of this approach to just-in-time creativity, problem solving and inspiring others is that it does not ask people to change forever.

And you can do this in 2 minutes or less, so this switch is also efficient and portable. I call this the 'dynamic switching loop' (see figure 5.4).

Let's look at an example.

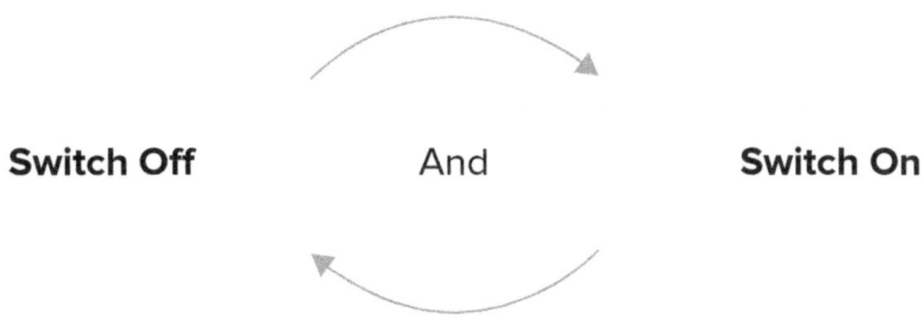

Figure 5.4 The dynamic switching loop

When you are facing a decision, you can, in 2 minutes:

- switch off analysis (e.g. pros and cons).
- switch on intuition (e.g. What does your gut feeling say?).

Now what happens? What do you experience? Play with the idea of just using your intuition. Perhaps you can also make a connection between what emerges from the switch off and the switch on states?

I use this microswitch all the time in my workshops and courses with amazing results. You can carry switch off and switch on around with you and use it anytime, anywhere with yourself, others and AI.

For example:

> *The situation:* You are paralysed by fear when asked to do something new.
> *Switch off:* a big leap.
> *Switch on:* a tiny, safe, concrete step.

You are now off and running with one small switch.

Switch off and switch on is the ideal way to learn and practise Switch Thinking in real time. You learn one specific experience at a time. Much like learning how to play golf, you start with the grip, then the stance, then hit a few balls and see what happens. You learn by doing.

You select a specific switch that you use for a few minutes without fear of failure. You just experiment and play.

Remember: the switch off and switch on is for 2 minutes only. You are disrupting your old thinking and accelerating a new way to think without fear. By switching off your usual Box Mode thinking you create space and time for new ideas, solutions or options to emerge.

And this is the key insight: to generate new thinking you need to switch off your old thinking.

A good example of this is what psychologists call 'functional fixedness'—the bias towards seeing an object in one way based on its widespread use or custom. For example, a laptop is typically used as a mobile information and communication device yet in an emergency it could be used as a weapon. The switch off & switch on technique encourages you to let go of a fixed view of seeing an object (or a situation or problem) and explore a different view.

The switch off and switch on technique is the ideal process when you are stuck, want to energise a group or give feedback on an idea. It's perfect for those moments when you need a change of direction quickly. Think of it as a HIIT workout for your brain (HIIT is 'high intensity interval training'). Short, fast thinking—it's a sprint, not a jog.

The great beauty of this skill is that you can use switch off and switch on anytime you need some new thinking with quite dramatic results.

Here's another example:

Switch off: using words to describe a new concept
Switch on: drawing it.

In my workshops participants have found this to be a fun, engaging and often insightful switch.

And it's so easy.

Switch off and switch on.

Repeat this to yourself whenever you are stuck. It does not matter what you switch off—you are creating space for a new possibility to emerge. Before you know it, you are starting to develop a switch off & switch on thinking habit and skill.

Say it out loud so others can adopt what you are doing.

For example:

Switch off: What are our differences?
Switch on: What do we have in common?

This is a simple switch to boost connection, collaboration, empathy and shared understanding.

And it's so easy to do. Consider this situation: You are struggling to build a connection with a colleague:

Switch off: Why are they being difficult?
Switch on: What might they be dealing with?

• • •

Switch off and switch on are small switches that give people a starting and ending point. I have found, paradoxically, that this helps people to think in a more open way. Rather than ask people to run as far as they can, you are asking them to run 20 metres, then stop and come back again. The switch off & switch on technique empowers people to open a new door in their mind knowing that their basic infrastructure is still in place.

The goal with switch off and switch on is to stop, or at least pause, what you always think, feel and do even if it is successful and consider another direction for just a few minutes. The switching back and forth not only develops your brain's neural agility but stops you from being fixed on an obvious solution.

The switch off and switch on technique works because you need to disrupt the usual to create the new. But the good news is that you can always switch back to what has worked in the past. It's just a small interruption in your thinking.

Another reason it works is that you are saying to yourself and others, 'we are switching off but we will soon switch back on'. It's not permanent; it's an exploration of a side track for a few moments to see what adventure awaits.

And what I have found is that most people are more likely to take a risk if they know they can switch back to what feels familiar and comfortable. Much like safety ropes are used in rock climbing. You can have all the excitement with a dollop of safety.

But here is the key point: with Switch Thinking you do not have to wait for an external event to switch what you think, feel and do. You can switch at any time.

Imagine if you could 'switch off and switch on', on demand! And use this whenever, wherever and with whomever you wanted to. It could be at work, home, at a dinner party, presentation, or working in a group or team. You would not have to wait for the right time, people or place.

Switch off Ball Mode and switch on Box Mode

Most of the examples I have been using have been suggestions to switch off Box Mode and switch on Ball Mode. This is because Box Mode is the usual starting place for most people (at work anyway).

However, you can also switch off your Ball Mode and switch on Box Mode.

For example:

Switch off: Procrastination.
Switch on: Making a first step, writing the first word—in 2 minutes you can create a mind map that outlines the main points in a presentation.

Another application is to use it to review your work. For example, I try to write as fast as I can so I don't listen to the doubts in my mind (e.g. will anyone be interested in this?). But this accelerated pace means I need to build in time to edit the work I produce. So, I:

Switch off: Generating anything new.
Switch on: A time for review.

This means I can produce quality work, quickly (most of the time!).

I was recently working at a café and the café owner said I seemed to be in my own bubble.

I replied, 'Yes, thank you'. I had:

Switched off: Noise.

Switched on: Focus.

Using the switch off and switch on process

The switch off and switch on process can be used with clients, colleagues, family members and teams.

You could, for example, be working with a colleague or a client and both switch off your current approach and switch on a different one.

Let's try it. In the next 2 minutes:

Switch off: How can we improve our sales by 5 per cent?

Switch on: What are some ideas to double our sales within 12 months?

Immediately, you both have to think differently—even if it's only for a few minutes—but in that time you might both come up with a breakthrough idea.

Or try this exercise with your team:

Switch off: Boring, long meetings.

Switch on: Meetings that anyone would love to attend.

Encourage your team to play with this idea. What new ideas emerge in 2 minutes?

The switch off and switch on process helps groups and teams to switch together. It builds movement, agility, curiosity and rhythm. It can build trust as you collectively switch off what might be still working to explore something new. Think of an orchestra where the string section starts, then switches off while the brass section takes over. Then they both come back together with the other sections (i.e. woodwinds and percussion) to perform a magnificent piece.

The switch on and switch off framework can enhance your team's culture. The language is not top down, heavy or permanent. It's light, inclusive and energising. Most of all, it gives all team members permission to experiment, play and have fun. It's safe, creative and productive.

It might also help your team to deal with stress. Let's switch off the pressure of generating results for a few minutes and check in with each other. Does anyone know a good joke or can anyone tell the team a fun thing they did on the weekend? Or let's just switch off this pace for a few minutes, take a breath and step back. How are we going? How is everyone feeling? Are we clear on what the next steps are?

Switch off and switch on with AI

You can also use switch off and switch on with AI and generate instant results. Most of us (at work) automatically slip into Box Mode. It's often our starting operating system. Why? Because we must deliver tangible results, achieve our goals, prioritise our time, budget and so on. AI is also designed to be efficient, accurate and based on predictability. Together, most of us and AI work in a linear, logical and structured way.

But this does not have to be the case.

Just as you can learn to switch off your automatic response to a situation, you can also develop this capability with your AI chatbot. Start by explaining what you are doing and why.

Here are some examples of switch off and switch on prompts you can use with AI:

> *Switch off:* The usual way of framing the problem.
> *Switch on:* 'Show me five radically different ways to reframe the problem'.

• • •

Switch off: A single correct answer.
Switch on: 'Give me four different answers — serious, playful, impossible and practical'.

• • •

Switch off: How to beat the competition?
Switch on: 'How can I co-create with our biggest competitor or a new startup?'

• • •

Switch off: The usual questions.
Switch on: 'What's a random question I have not asked?'

• • •

Switch off: Any solution that has worked before.
Switch on: 'An original solution'.

• • •

With these examples you are giving AI more than just a prompt. You are creating a new expectation and encouraging it to move beyond the automatic.

Why does switch off and switch on work?

Switch off and switch on works for several reasons.

It gives the creativity process a structure

Many leaders want their team to be more innovative and so they ask them to go in the corner and be creative. This sounds good, but is not very helpful. How do you do this when you have not been taught to do it?

This is where the switch off and switch on idea works beautifully. There is freedom within limits: a 2-minute time limit and a guide so you know what to switch off and what to switch on. For example:

Switch off: Trying to make our current solution better.
Switch on: What is the ideal solution?

This simple switch can help you unlock your individual and collective imagination. Remember: there is no right or wrong—you are just playing with what could exist for a few minutes.

You can step outside of yourself

Switch off and switch on is a quick, effective way to consider the perspectives of others. This can lead to greater understanding and empathy.

Switch off: What's my perspective of this situation?
Switch on: What's your perspective (or your goals, dreams, ambitions, etc.)?

This framing means you can bypass your own defensiveness. You don't feel attacked; you are genuinely trying to understand someone else's perspective.

It's often easier to be open when you don't have to give up your position—you are just switching it off for a moment.

Here's another example that can help develop greater understanding and collaboration:

Switch off: Listening to the extroverts.
Switch on: Encouraging the introverts.

Again, use this switch for just a few minutes. You might find, however, that when you make this switch you learn more by listening than articulating your views. This approach also means you can put your ego aside for a few moments. This switch is reflected here:

> *Switch off:* What you know.
> *Switch on:* What you don't know.

It helps you interrupt your automatic thinking patterns

The switch off and switch on technique encourages you and others to pause and interrupt your usual, traditional approach.

For example:

> *Switch off:* Solving the problem (the usual approach).
> *Switch on:* Preventing the problem.

These switches disrupt your default thinking patterns in a simple, direct way. 'Rather than solving a problem, how do I prevent it?' Asking 'Why not?' rather than always asking 'Why?' might open a more solution-oriented individual and collective mindset.

It enables you to access your imagination

Your usual Box Mode starting point is to consider what has worked before and build on that. But what if you considered a more imaginative approach?

> *Switch off:* What has worked before?
> *Switch on:* What's never been tried before?

This switch invites a more open and playful approach. You do not have to be sensible, logical or reasonable. You are just using your imagination for a few minutes.

Suddenly, you can consider the unimaginable:

Switch off: What's possible?
Switch on: What's impossible?

It's such a great switch.

Driverless cars or drones in combat were once considered impossible. But now technology is the enabler of our individual and collective imagination. People who usually feel constrained by reason or fear of failure suddenly have permission to play.

The 'switch' makes it safe to be a bit silly, to explore the impossible, to laugh. This is freeing and expansive. It can bring back the childlike mode of exploration that adults often suppress in professional settings.

Switching off the constant internal chatter allows your DMN to re-engage your insight, imagination and reflection (i.e. what I call being in Ball Mode).

It helps you remove your fear of judgement

What stops most of us from being as creative as we possibly can be? Often, it's the fear of failure, judgement or making a mistake.

But what if you could take this away even for a few minutes. Imagine what you could create, feel and do?

Switch off: Being fearful.
Switch on: Being fearless.

It's empowering.

What if you didn't worry about what others thought of you. Wouldn't that be empowering?

Switch off: What I am not good at?
Switch on: What I am awesome at?

2-minute Switch Thinking exercise

Carry a switch ball with you

I carry a ball with me all the time in my backpack. I often use it when I, or the group I am working with, is stuck. The ball, of course, represents Ball Mode. It immediately lightens up your spirit and brings a playful smile to your face.

Hold the ball in your right hand and, when faced with a challenge or problem, squeeze the ball as you generate a few ideas. This represents Box Mode. For most people, it's their preferred, stronger hand and represents their CEN (assuming you are right-handed).

Now switch the ball to your left hand. This is (for most people) your weaker hand. Try tossing the ball up and down in your left hand as you generate some new ideas. This will feel slightly uncomfortable but will command your attention. Your left-hand action represents your DMN (assuming you are right-handed). Don't filter any of your ideas—let them flow.

After a few minutes, roll the ball back and forth between your right and left hand. This represents the idea of connecting your Box Mode with your Ball Mode ideas.

Playing with a ball is a simple, beautiful way to embed being able to switch your thinking in a physical action. You will never view a ball the same way again.

Chapter 6

Prompt imagining

Most of us interact with AI by using one of the AI chatbots via a series of prompts — for example, *Can you write a job application letter aimed at the human resource director of a particular company?* It's amazingly quick, valuable and, most of the time, accurate (even allowing for a few blips along the way). And AI can learn and improve, the more information we feed it.

In short, AI is here to stay and can only get better.

The interaction with AI is called 'prompt engineering'. Indeed, there are courses on how to use prompts in the right way to achieve the right outcomes.

But let's step back a moment (notice I paused). Prompt engineering was developed by software engineers to make this interaction with AI fast, efficient and productive. But when I think of an engineer, words such as 'structure', 'precision', 'reason' and 'logic' pop into my head.

Prompt engineering is what I describe as being in a Box Mode loop (see figure 6.1, overleaf). You think in Box Mode, prompt in this mode and AI responds in this mode.

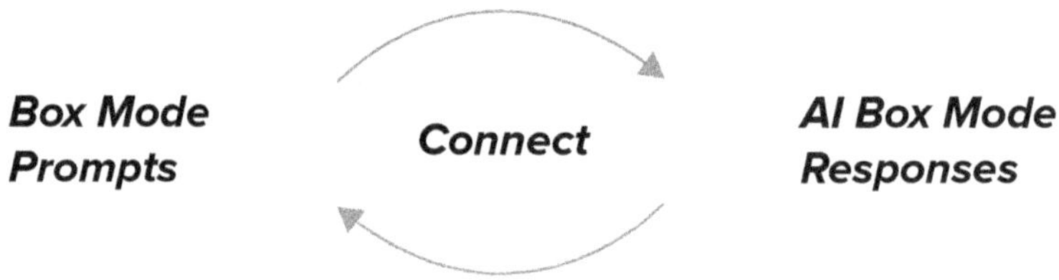

Figure 6.1 The Box Mode loop

This type of prompting can be fast and efficient. I regularly use AI to summarise, to evaluate and as a powerful research tool. Its great strength is the use of logic and analysis. This can save time, effort and money.

The disadvantages of prompting in Box Mode

One of the issues of being in Box Mode is that you can over-rely on AI for one of your most important skills: your ability to think critically. This should always remain a human skill that is enhanced by AI not replaced by it. How would you know if AI is indeed correct if you cannot think critically about its responses?

Another issue with prompt engineering is that it is predictive. This is very efficient. AI has learned that when I type in 'Sw', for example, it most likely means that I am about to type in 'switch'. This saves me time and effort.

However, this very strength means that AI (and our own mind) tend to respond based on previous experience. This predictive patterning is logical and linear but can lock you into existing thinking structures rather than exploring something using a more unstructured approach.

This can mean that if you are in Box Mode you will tend to ask Box Mode prompts and receive Box Mode responses. This creates a self-reinforcing cycle and can be limiting in a rapidly changing world, which means you can get stuck. The results will be safe and incremental rather than generating a breakthrough idea. For example, I am eating my porridge this morning topped with banana. This brings back lovely memories of holidaying down the coast and going for a surf then having a banana smoothie with friends. This in turn triggers an idea of perhaps inventing a recipe to eat before swimming that might reduce your chances of being attacked by a shark. Notice I started with porridge and bananas and my imaginative mind ended up not being eaten by a shark—quite a non-linear thought process that would be unlikely if you stick to Box Mode prompts only.

Using only Box Mode prompts might also mean that your competitors are prompting AI with the same structured, logical prompts and receiving much the same responses. This is another reason why it is a good idea to use a number of AI chatbots when you are working on a problem. As each will have different data sets, you might get slightly different responses.

It is for these reasons that I am suggesting you use a different way to prompt AI that can co-exist with prompt engineering.

I call this 'prompt imagining'.

It does not replace, but rather complements, your existing interactions with AI. Think *and* not *or*. The great news is that it can be done with humans and AI at any time (see figure 6.2).

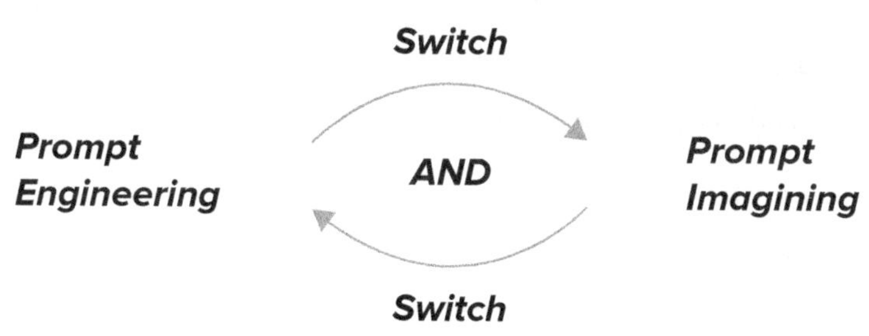

Figure 6.2 Prompt engineering *and* prompt imagining

The goal of prompt imagining, as the name suggests, is to create, imagine, stretch and challenge your and AI's existing default thinking. The focus is on creating difference rather than accuracy (this is the role of Box Mode prompting).

It's a conscious, deliberate switch to Ball Mode prompting.

By doing so you can create a powerful contrast with prompt engineering, which can be exciting and insightful. The magic is in the interactions between the two different types of prompts and the results that follow. It's the creative tension and possible connections that might emerge from operating in Box Mode and Ball Mode supercharged by AI.

Switching to Ball Mode prompts can also mean you might generate a new idea or solution that surprises your competitors, customers and team.

For example:

Prompt engineering: How might you describe Switch Thinking in 50 words or less?

AI responded with: Switch Thinking is a two-mode framework for improving creativity and problem solving by switching between Box Mode and imaginative Ball Mode to generate new ideas and solutions in 2 minutes or less.

This response makes perfect sense. And as the inventor of Switch Thinking, I can tell you that it is entirely accurate, factual and predictable.

However, I also asked a different Ball Mode prompt:

Prompt imagining: Can you describe Switch Thinking using a metaphor?

AI responded with: Switch Thinking is like breathing for the mind: you inhale structure, exhale imagination and the rhythm between them keeps your ideas alive.

As you can see, this is quite a different response — which I love. It's evocative, memorable and surprising. And what is remarkable is that it comes from the same AI (i.e. ChatGPT) — just different prompts asked at much the same time.

With prompt imagining the goal is not accuracy but exploration, play and possibility. There is no right or wrong prompt (or response) you can use. In fact, the more random the prompt the better.

Prompt imagining gives you permission to ask AI all sorts of interesting questions without worrying about the accuracy of the responses. You are looking for difference and originality with these types of prompts.

For example:

Prompt engineering: What are the three major causes of inequality?

vs

Prompt imagining: How might a painter communicate the idea of inequality to politicians?

As you can see in these examples, with prompt imagining the goal becomes less an instruction and more of a creative spark. You are proactively providing new stimulus for AI to respond. It's what I like to term the Ball Mode AI loop (see figure 6.3).

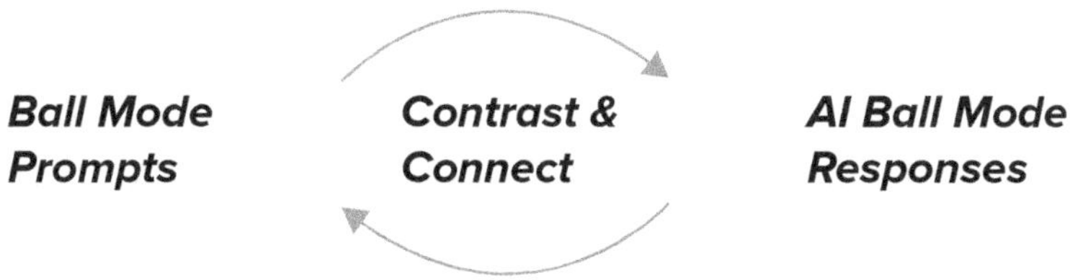

Figure 6.3 The Ball Mode AI loop

Prompt imagining places more of the emphasis on how we ask AI, which in turn dictates how AI responds. This means that we are co-creating with AI. This generates a positive creating cycle or loop.

Your human creativity is pushing AI, which in turn is responding and perhaps challenging you to think differently.

This human and AI cycle using prompt imagining can be playful, fun and open ended.

For example:

Prompt engineering: Can you give me 10 reasons why teams fail?

Prompt imagining: Why might a pride of lions turn on each other?

Notice these prompts are asking much the same question yet in a completely different way. Your AI will no doubt respond in a fact-based way to the first prompt and hopefully in a more imaginative way to the second prompt.

Connecting prompt engineering with prompt imagining

If you are in Box Mode and switch to Ball Mode you increase your chances of developing a breakthrough idea or solution quickly.

But a more advanced method is to try and connect the responses from the prompt engineering approach with those from prompt imagining.

This means you can have the best of both worlds. Imagination and practicality powered by AI.

For example:

Prompt engineering: What are three strategies a professional freelancer (working by themselves) can use to win new clients?

AI response: Create an online portfolio, ask for referrals, post thought leadership content.

Then I asked basically the same question but in a more imaginative (Ball Mode) way.

Prompt imagining: Harley is our six-year-old golden retriever: cuddly, affectionate and protective. How could Harley help a professional freelancer win new clients?
AI response: Be like Harley: greet people warmly, listen attentively, show genuine care and build consistency and trust.
My connecting prompt: Using Harley's playful, loyal approach as inspiration, what are three specific strategies a freelancer could use to build trust and connection with potential clients?

AI response:

1. Send a personalised 'welcome' message to new clients that's warm and human, not corporate.
2. Follow up with curiosity: ask thoughtful questions to show genuine interest in their goals.
3. Offer small gestures of appreciation (a thank-you note, a free resource, or a kind referral) that make clients feel valued and remembered.

The great news is that this entire interaction took less than 2 minutes. It was fast, enjoyable and insightful. Often, you only need one idea to make a big difference.

Importantly, I had moved beyond prompt engineering (i.e. Box Mode) to prompt imagining (i.e. Ball Mode). It was a switch from a sensible, rational approach to something more creative and collaborative.

Working with AI in this way is fast, fun, exploratory and non-judgemental. The language becomes more human and often insightful. It can also set up a lovely contrast with the prompt engineering approach.

ChatGPT summarised this interaction for me: 'Prompt engineering helps you talk to AI clearly. Prompt imagining helps you think with

AI creatively. It's not about getting the perfect output; it's about discovering new ways of seeing the world'.

The other benefit of prompt imagining is that it helps my creativity to soar. The simple act of pausing and trying to develop a more imaginative prompt enhances and stretches my (and others') thinking. It forces me to think beyond the usual approach. This is a creative act in itself. Ironically, AI is encouraging me to be more creative so it can be more imaginative. A true co-creating cycle.

The development of a new Ball Mode prompt switches my thinking from Box Mode to Ball Mode automatically. It does so in a semi-structured way that most people find comfortable. It's like switch off and switch on in that you are using a technique that is fast, simple and easy to communicate and demonstrate to others.

Remember: it's not prompt engineering or prompt imagining. It's when they are used together that the full potential of this approach is realised. For example, you can post on LinkedIn, Facebook and TikTok with limited results, yet the moment you add an image or video your results can often multiply. It's the interaction and connection that makes the difference. Michael Jordan, for example, was one of the greatest basketball players not just because of his attacking prowess but also because he was a dominant defender.

It's prompt engineering (i.e. Box Mode) × prompt imagining (i.e. Ball Mode).

Here's an example.

My ChatGPT prompt: 'What are the benefits of prompt imagining?'
ChatGPT responded:

- It can activate your default mode network.
- It creates more vivid, inspiring and meaningful outputs.
- It reduces blank-page syndrome.
- It helps bypass fear, perfectionism and over-thinking.

- It encourages rapid iteration.
- It unlocks lateral, non-linear solutions.

However, I then switched to a prompt imagining approach by asking the same question in a different way:

> *My ChatGPT prompt:* 'What are the benefits of prompt imagining so even kids would love it?'
> *ChatGPT responded:* 'Imagine you have a magic talking robot. And imagine that this robot is SUPER smart, but it only becomes fun, creative and magical when you start imagining first'.

That's prompt imagining. It turns AI into a magical playmate rather than something to be frightened of. It can become a collaborator and a co-creator. I have found that using prompt imagining gives me creative confidence. It pushes my thinking into new areas that I might not venture into by myself. And it helps me take more risks with my thinking as I can bypass my often-critical inner voice saying 'You might be wrong or what might others say' because I am interacting with AI at a fast pace.

Here are some examples of prompt imagining:

- Imagine the question is a maze. How might our team escape this maze?
- How might using LEGO bricks help me solve this problem?
- What questions might the world's most curious person ask right now?

Prompt imagining removes fear and adds fun to any challenge. I feel my own creativity muscle getting stronger when I use this approach. It's training my DMN in real time. This means that in moments that matter I can instantly switch to a new way of thinking.

This might be the biggest benefit.

Human creativity × technology

One of the great attractions of London is called ABBA Voyage. It's a show that combines the classic songs of Swedish group ABBA with digital avatars, cutting-edge lighting and a purpose-built arena and you have a show and an experience that are second to none.

I have been, and I must confess that about 20 minutes into the performance I had to remind myself that there were avatars on stage, not the real ABBA members.

I love this example of how technology multiplied by human creativity can produce wondrous results. The ABBA group members are well into their senior years, so the idea of touring was not really possible.

But, switching to Ball Mode, perhaps the original producers of the show asked different questions, such as:

- What if our performance could be reimagined, not repeated?
- What if a concert isn't about physical presence but emotional presence?

I do not know the back story, but you can see how these types of questions could lead to the development of ABBA Voyage, a groundbreaking virtual concert.

This is just a tiny example of the creative potential I believe awaits humans and AI. Of course, there are issues to be worked through with AI in terms of privacy, intellectual property and hallucinations but the models are improving. There are also issues around using AI for military purposes (and the like) that cannot be dismissed. But my optimistic view is that tools such as Switch Thinking powered by AI can unleash unimaginable solutions to large-scale problems such as loneliness, climate tracking, healthcare and education, to name just a few.

The key is to start now. Start playing with AI by using prompt engineering and the awesome potential of prompt imagining.

2-minute Switch Thinking exercise

The next time you use your generative AI and it responds, *pause*.

Then ask your AI to respond to the same prompt from one of these perspectives:

- a dog catcher
- the lead singer in a band
- a child with reading difficulties
- an astronaut.

What new ideas or insights emerge?

For fun, ask your AI to try to connect the responses from your two different prompts.

What magical ideas emerge?

Try a different perspective next time. Do this a few times and it can become your new, more imaginative way to interact with AI.

Pause

I have always liked the idea of an intermission. As you know, it's a pause, or a short break, in a play, concert or film.

So why not a book?

In this break I wanted to quickly recap where we have come from and what lies ahead.

Recap

Let's think about tennis as an analogy to talk about the ideas we have covered to date with Switch Thinking.

You have started playing your opponent with a plan in place. Perhaps stay at the baseline, rely on your groundstrokes and wait for a mistake. It's worked before and you are comfortable with this approach. Halfway through the match, your opponent can predict what you are going to do. The points are getting shorter and you feel the match is slipping away.

This is a key moment in the game. Do you stick to your plan or try something new? (See figure P.1.)

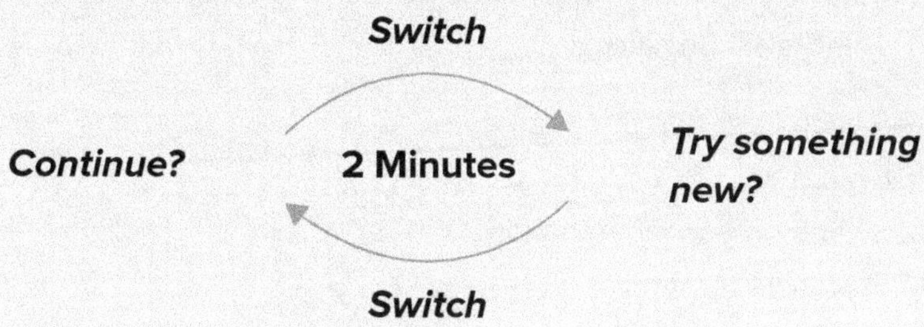

Figure P.1 Pause: Is it working or time to switch?

This is the essence of Switch Thinking. You pause, recognise the moment and consider a switch to a different way of thinking, feeling and acting for a few minutes. In the tennis example, you might try coming to the net or slowing the pace of your shots, for example. Or you can continue with your plan and hope that something changes.

In moving slightly outside your comfort zone (i.e. your original plan), you are challenging yourself and you may become more competent in another part of the game and hence improve overall.

What's also powerful about this metaphor is that the pause and switch happen in real time, during the game, not before or after. This requires awareness of a situation, not more effort, and you can influence the result in minutes. This example also highlights the idea that you can switch back at any time.

This is Switch Thinking in action. You are learning a new mindset and language that can unleash your full thinking potential during an event, experience or interaction.

What lies ahead

To continue your journey, the next stage is to learn some specific switches.

I call these '6 switches'.

I have developed and tested these switches with hundreds of leaders and their teams on all sorts of challenges.

The 6 switches are:

1. Switch your perspective
2. Switch your focus
3. Switch on your imagination
4. Switch your emotion
5. Switch your rules
6. Switch your questions.

There is no limit to the number of switches you can use. Try one, then move on to another. Use as many or as few as you wish.

There is no right or wrong way to use these switches.

You can use any of the switches in any order, by yourself with a team or co-creating with AI. The switch you select can be a matter of personal preference or the challenge at hand.

To illustrate how these switches might work independently and together, let's take the example of a chair. (Why a chair? Simply a random choice and it's an everyday item.)

The chair is a metaphor for any problem, challenge, issue, career, project or even your career. The following Switch Thinking example will show how a small switch in thinking can help you see even an everyday object like a chair in a new way using the 6 switches.

Psychologists call this tendency or cognitive bias to only see an object based on its intended or traditional use, 'functional fixedness' (hence a chair is to sit on—right?).

Let's take each of the 6 switches (see figure P.2) and see what happens if you make a small switch in how you think about a chair.

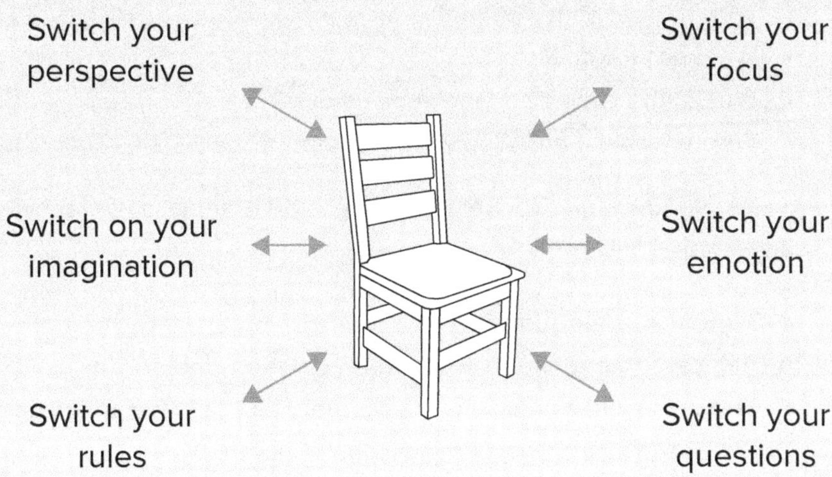

Figure P.2 The 6 switches

1 Switch your perspective

A chair looks different depending on who's looking at it. For example, an interior designer sees style, lines, form and how it fits a room. A parent with toddlers, by comparison, sees safety, sharp edges, stability and hazards. A cat sees a home.

Switching your perspective means you can look at the same object but see different things.

2 Switch your focus

You can focus on the size, weight, height, cost, comfort or material. By switching focus, you switch meaning and by switching meaning, you switch possibilities.

3 Switch on your imagination

You can use 'What if?' to open doors that your rational mind usually keeps shut. For example:

- What if the chair were alive? What stories would it tell?
- Who has sat on it?
- What has it witnessed?
- What if the chair could move on its own?
- Where would it go? Who would it help?

Switching to imagination restores play—the birthplace of creativity and innovation.

4 Switch your emotion

A chair can change dramatically when emotion is added.

This is not just a chair—it was your late mother's favourite chair. Or this chair reminds me of my childhood home.

Switching to emotions can reveal hidden significance and influence behaviour far more than logic alone. Emotions uncover why the chair matters.

5 Switch your rules (e.g. assumptions)

This switch asks you to challenge your beliefs, conventions or hidden assumptions behind the chair (and hence any problem). For example:

- Why does a chair need four legs? Could it have six?
- Does a chair have to be owned? Could it be shared or temporary?
- Must all chairs around a table look the same? Why can't they all be different?

Switching rules reveals how often our thinking is trapped inside invisible boundaries—and how freeing it feels to challenge them.

6 Switch your questions

A chair becomes far more interesting when you change the question:

- Do we need a chair at all? What would a 'standing chair' look like?
- What could we call it instead? A 'body-holder'? A 'rest device'?

The quality of your questions determines the quality of possibilities you see. Switching your questions changes the future you can imagine.

Notice how easy these switches are? A small switch using any of these 6 switches can make a big difference in a very short time.

Remember: the chair can represent any situation, problem or opportunity. You do not have to be constrained in your thinking just because something has worked in the past.

You can choose to switch.

When you do, you can open your mind (and those of others) to a magical way of being that is filled with hope, optimism, empathy, understanding and creativity.

In the next six chapters, I'll deep dive into each of the 6 switches in turn.

Chapter 7

Switch your perspective

I can still remember the day of my eldest daughter's 12th birthday party. She wanted a horse-riding party — of course!

I organised the venue, food and drinks and picked up a flock of 12 years olds for the big event. Exhausted, I sat down and waved goodbye to the first rider as I looked forward to a well-earned cup of tea.

'Dad, are you coming?'

'Of course', I said (what choice did I have?). The organisers duly trotted out what I thought was the biggest horse in the stables. The horse and I spied each other and decided that neither of us was comfortable — so I swallowed some pride and said that I could not go.

And yet ...

The more I looked at the horse, the more I decided that, really, the horse was just a big dog.

I love dogs.

Instant calm for both me and my rather large friend.

Well, to my surprise I trotted off and quite enjoyed myself with body and pride intact.

The moral of the story?

The horse had not changed ... but I had. I had perceived the situation differently (i.e. the horse as a big dog), which in turn changed how I felt (i.e. more relaxed) and what I did (i.e. enjoyed the ride).

This is an everyday example that illustrates the power of being able to see any situation differently. It's fast, immediate and often insightful. What's more, many people have told me in my workshops that switching your perspective is the easiest of the 6 switches to use.

Why is 'switch your perspective' easy to use?

In the business world, managers are encouraged to view any situation from the customer or user perspective, so this concept is not entirely new (although not always practised, in my experience). Switching your perspective is familiar and encouraged in many fields, especially service-oriented ones. It is also used extensively in movies and TV series — for example, the World War II drama, *Band of Brothers* (2001) uses a different member of Easy Company 506th Parachute Infantry Regiment for each of its 10 episodes. This creates a dramatic narrative through the entire series.

Here are some business examples of switching perspective:

- What is a competitor perspective?
  Switch.
  What is a startup perspective?
- What is a profit perspective?
  Switch.
  What is a sustainability perspective?

The key I have found with switching perspectives is that it opens your thinking quickly and the ideas flowing from both perspectives provide a potential new connection and stronger solution (think *and* not *or*). As Alan Kay (one of the early pioneers of modern personal computing) suggested, 'A new perspective is worth at least 80 IQ points'.

> The next time you have to make a decision, ask yourself:
>
> *What is a head perspective?*
>
> (e.g. What will make the most money?)
>
> *Switch.*
>
> *What is a heart perspective?*
>
> (e.g. What is consistent with my values?)
>
> Using these two perspectives can help you make a better, well-rounded decision.

Switching your perspective is creative, empathetic and often insightful. I once designed a café from the perspective of a child. This opened my eyes (and the café owner's, who asked me to do it) to questions such as:

- Who should be served first? (the child)
- Who should the café employ? (people who like kids)
- What should it look like? (loud, fun, playful)

Another wonderful advantage of switching your perspective is that it doesn't require special tools, deep training or a whiteboard — it's something you can do in a café, at home or in the middle of a conversation.

It also doesn't feel too personal or risky. Like an actor in a play or movie, you can try on any number of perspectives. They are neither right nor wrong — just different. In fact, you can ground a risky perspective with a safe one. This can set up opportunities to make new connections.

It's also quick. You can shift your perspective in seconds. This is ideal in those moments where you need to respond to a conversation that has suddenly gone off the rails.

Pause and ask yourself:

- What is their perspective?
- How are they seeing this situation?
- Is it aligned with how I am seeing the same situation?

You can pivot and say, 'Just so I understand what you are saying, can I summarise?' This is not ageing or disagreeing, but clarifying by the use of a simple switch of perspective.

When you switch your perspective, you don't need a deep process or long setup. It's intuitive and often spontaneous. This can lead to a deeper understanding and even help you consider other points of view in crafting a better idea or action.

Switching your perspective is also a powerful way to boost your empathy. Rather than ruminate on why your partner is being difficult, you can switch and see the situation from their perspective and perhaps better understand what they might be dealing with.

Before a presentation I always try to switch to the perspective of my audience:

- What are they looking for?
- What will their concerns be?
- How can I address their issues in a compelling way?

This switching of perspective not only applies in a formal presentation but also when you are dealing with, say, a flatmate who is making too much noise. You could ask yourself, 'What are they thinking and feeling when they play loud music?' Perhaps they don't realise that their music is too loud.

While this doesn't always resolve the situation, it does lead to better understanding.

Another advantage of switching your perspective is that it creates psychological distance. One of the most interesting observations I have found in my workshops is that when someone says, 'This is how so-and-so might see it…', they're removing personal responsibility.

If the idea flops, it's not their failure — it's so-and-so's 'crazy' idea.

This makes it safer to explore the wild, weird or wonderful and reduces the fear of judgement.

Speaking through a character, role or archetype gives people emotional cover. They're not being silly or radical — they're being in character. For example, 'I'm not proposing this. I'm just channelling Rihanna'.

Another advantage of switching your perspective is that it can open up new opportunities to develop new products, services or experiences for your customers or clients.

The situation: How might an experienced theatregoer react to the latest play?

Switch: How might someone seeing their very first play react?

The seasoned theatre goers might enjoy some in-depth reading about the background to the play, the actors, director and how it differs from other productions. The second group might appreciate some notes on what to expect in a play more generally, what to look for and some suggestions on the storyline.

How to use Switch your perspective

The starting point is to pause and ask yourself, 'What thinking mode does the moment call for?'

Then ask yourself (or others in a team), 'What mode are you in now? Box Mode or Ball Mode?'

If you are in Box Mode, your goal in switching your perspective is to break free from your (and others') habitual or go-to paths and develop potentially new shortcuts in your mind. It doesn't matter, therefore, which perspective you use.

This is a key point: you can adopt any new or different perspective, and it will help you interrupt your current patterns. It could be a dentist, gardener or a pilot flying a jumbo jet. The goal is the same.

In fact, I have found that the more random the perspective, the greater the chance that you will come up with an original idea. When you switch your perspective, randomness is your friend.

Once you are adept at switching perspectives, try connecting. Use a different perspective to see a situation in a new way and then try to connect your ideas from your usual perspective to the new one. It's these interactions that can often lead to breakthrough solutions that connect ideas in new ways. In figure 7.1 you can see how easily you can switch perspectives from the usual to a new one.

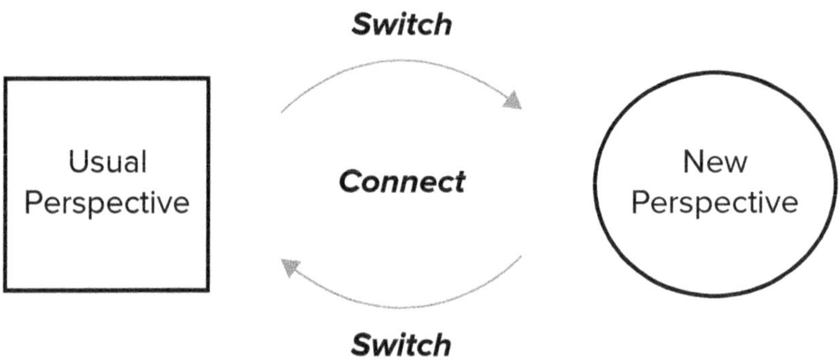

Figure 7.1 Switching and connecting perspectives

A simple way anyone can switch on their creativity

One of my tennis friends confided in me one day that he did not have a creative bone in his body.

After our usual doubles game, I asked him how a (friendly) clown might make tennis more fun.

'Perhaps each court could be painted in a different colour', he said. Then, warming to the task, 'Every player could wear a funny hat, perhaps music plays in the background and a prerecorded cheer goes off after a great shot'.

He could not stop.

I asked him what he was doing.

'Creating', he said.

Yes, creating big, beautiful ideas — in minutes!

Just by switching his perspective.

Related or random perspectives?

Let's imagine you need to develop a new employee retention strategy. It makes sense to consider an employee's or a recent graduate's perspective.

These are perspectives related to the problem at hand. But sometimes these do not go far enough. In a sense, these are still Box Mode perspectives.

To create more original ideas and possibilities that stand out, you need to switch to a random Ball Mode perspective.

For example:

- How might a music conductor look at this situation?
- Or a veterinarian?
- Or Greta Thunberg?

As a team leader you might develop a retention strategy based on not just performance but also values. Your efforts might become more focused on retaining those team members who excel at their job and have values that are aligned with the organisation.

Or perhaps the best way to retain staff (paradoxically) is to encourage them to take 12 months off and work in a sustainable, not-for-profit or environmental agency (thanks, Greta Thunberg, for this lens). They can then return with a much broader view of work, relationships and life.

These random perspectives help you switch to Ball Mode and engage your DMN. Then, if you amplify this process with AI, you can really stretch your mind and expand your solution space.

Then you can switch back to Box Mode and evaluate your big, new, random ideas.

How to use with AI

Switching perspective using AI is fun and easy. Let's take the same challenge: how to develop a more engaging employee retention strategy. Start in Box Mode and prompt your AI to generate some initial ideas, and determine a timeline and budget.

Now let's switch to Ball Mode using a veterinarian's perspective. Why a vet? Purely random.

Using this example, I prompted AI to give me three new ideas using a vet's perspective. This is what happened:

1. *Regular wellness checks (not just performance reviews)*
   Just like vets do routine checkups to prevent problems before they escalate, introduce monthly 'check-ins' that focus on emotional, mental and career wellbeing — not just key performance indicators.

2. *Tailored care plans*
   Veterinarians create individualised a care plan for each animal. Apply this by designing personalised growth or motivation plans for employees based on their 'working temperament', interests and aspirations.
3. *Recognition by species (or style)*
   Some pets respond to treats, others to praise or play. Do the same with employees: identify different 'appreciation languages' and recognise each person in the way that most resonates with them.

Next, I switched back to Box Mode and asked AI to evaluate my ideas based on cost, feasibility and potential engagement. I could also have tried to connect some of AI's ideas with my own to develop an even bigger, better solution.

What happens if you start in Ball Mode?

Sometimes you might be in Ball Mode, such as in a brainstorming session, or because it's your preferred or starting style. In these situations, you can still switch your perspective to Box Mode with ease and gain an immediate benefit. If you start in Ball Mode, as in figure 7.2, you can switch back to Box Mode at any time.

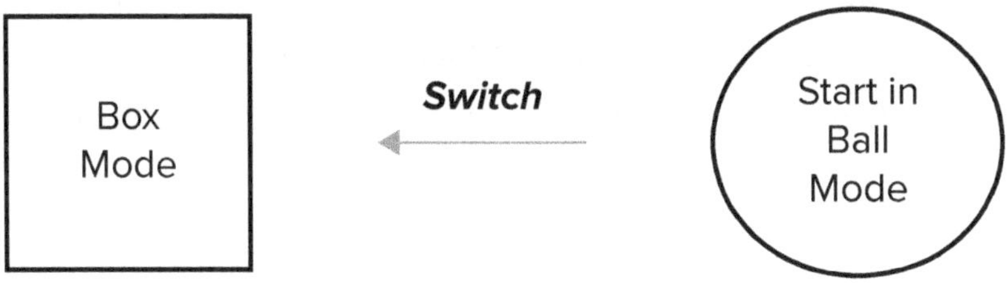

Figure 7.2 Switch to Box Mode

If you are in Ball Mode, you can switch to a Box Mode perspective for 2 minutes. This could be a project manager, engineer or financial controller perspective.

From this perspective some of the aspects you might focus on are:

- Do we have the budget for this?
- What are the next steps?
- What can we achieve in the next 30 days?
- Will this idea help me or us achieve our goals?

Switching back to Box Mode (either human or using AI) can give you a greater sense of structure, planning and control. And remember: with all the switches, it's not permanent. Use this switch if it is useful, then switch back.

The advantages of switching your perspective

Being able to switch your perspective on demand is fast, easy and can make a big difference in minutes. This is the ideal switch when you are stuck or you mind freezes. It can be used anywhere, anytime, by yourself or with a group, team or with AI.

Another benefit is that it formalises what many people are doing already. This makes it easy to practise and show others.

Switching your perspective can also work both ways from Box Mode to Ball Mode and from Ball Mode to Box Mode. This makes it versatile and dynamic. It's your key switch for developing a more agile and creative mind.

Switching your perspective also encourages play, experimentation and imagination. You can take greater risks when you adopt someone else's perspective and it helps you experience a situation with greater understanding.

Switching your perspective is also a fun exercise to do with a group or team. Someone can adopt the perspective of, say, a plumber, a chef or a superhero. You do this for a few minutes, then discuss your insights. There is no limit to the number of perspectives you can adopt, nor is there a right or wrong one. It's just a different way of seeing a situation.

When you switch your perspective, you open a permission gate. Often, people are sitting on great ideas, but they don't feel they have permission to share them. Perspective-switching grants that permission — for example, 'It's not me saying this... but what if we cancelled the whole project and started again?'

Another benefit of switching your perspective is that it builds empathy and understanding in others. You are genuinely trying to see the world in their shoes. This may not always lead to a positive outcome, but it certainly is a better starting point.

2-minute Switch Thinking exercise

Adopt the perspective of someone else at a meeting

I once heard a golf professional suggest that after you have hit your shot you should imagine what shot your playing partners might play around the green (e.g. a high lob or a pitch and run).

She was trying to expand my golf imagination in real time.

What if you adopted the same idea at your next meeting or presentation? Try to become each of the other people for a few moments. How are they looking at this situation? What are their issues or hot buttons? When they reply, how close were you?

I do this all the time to exercise my switch perspective muscle and to gain insights from the other people at the table (this is ideal for anyone who is presenting, selling or pitching an idea).

Chapter 8

Switch your focus

A few years ago, my wife and I went to see the Tom Cruise movie *Top Gun: Maverick*. We both saw the same movie, at the same time, yet had very different experiences. I loved the action scenes, but my wife was more concerned with 'the arc of the leading female character'.

We both enjoyed the movie despite focusing on different aspects.

Not good or bad — just different.

Switch your focus is the second of my 6 switches. If Switching your perspective is the 'how you see a situation', then Switch your focus is the 'what, where and when' of any situation.

> Think back to the last time you had a disagreement with someone. What was your focus? Was it on the disagreement itself, the relationship or your emotion?

Your focus

Where, when and what you focus your attention on is largely dependent on your previous thinking patterns. You tend to pay attention to what you have always paid attention to.

Why?

Because in most situations it has worked for you.

For example, when you are presented with a table of sales numbers you might focus on the longer term trends or the profit margin or the results of your biggest customers.

It does not mean that the other sales information is not important, but you have learned through experience that most of what you need from a page of numbers is contained in a few figures.

There is a self-reinforcing quality to this process. You focus on aspects in your environment that have worked in the past. This is efficient and ensures that you are not overwhelmed with information.

Box Mode focus

Box Mode is fast, easy and comfortable. It's often your default mode of thinking.

However, it can blind you to other aspects of any situation because you only ever see part of any landscape.

For example, in my previous life I worked in marketing for American Express. Our focus was on acquiring new cardmembers at an acceptable cost. What we didn't focus on was how many cardmembers were leaving the business. This created a leaky bucket. We were pouring in money to acquire customers instead of those who were leaving. When we switched our focus from acquiring to developing and retaining cardmembers our business profitability started to really take off.

The lesson?

You can focus on different aspects of any situation and by doing so you can open your mind and create opportunities that you might have never seen before.

Ball Mode focus

Ball Mode focus is the idea of deliberately focusing on a different part of a situation, problem or opportunity.

With a Ball Mode focus there is no good or bad place to focus — the goal is to switch to a different one. The good news is that you have more agency over what you focus on than you realise.

You can't always change the situation — but you can always switch your focus.

Here's an example:

- You can focus on the sale.
  Switch.
  You can focus on the relationship.
- You can focus on what you know.
  Switch.
  You can focus on what you don't know.

The key point is that there is no right or wrong way to focus.

You have a choice.

You can continue to focus on the same things, in the same way.

Pause.

Or you can switch your focus and open new possibilities, options and actions.

Often, the secret sauce is in the interaction and iteration between your usual focus and a different one. As you can see in figure 8.1 (overleaf), you can switch back and forth between your usual focus and a different one.

When you focus on something different you may notice something hidden — perhaps a new opportunity or understanding of a situation.

There is no end to what you can focus on.

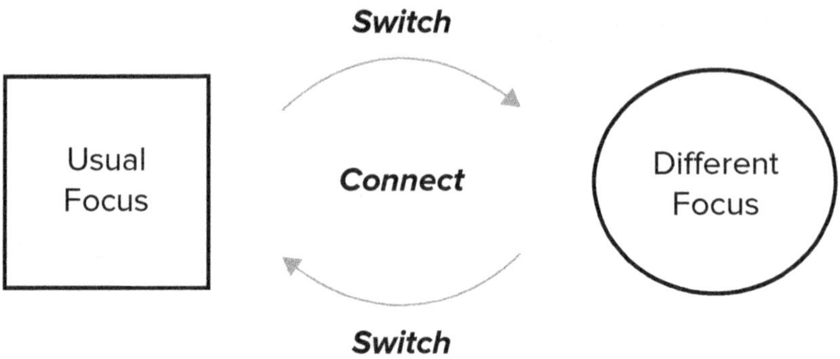

Figure 8.1 Switching your focus

> What am I focused on right now?
> What else could I choose to focus on?

When faced with a problem or a situation, often your usual focus is, 'What's not working?' or 'What am I doing wrong?'

This focus will limit your range of possible solutions.

This focus is still valuable, of course. However, you can also switch your focus:

Usual focus: What is not working?
Switch.
Different focus: What is working well? *or* What am I doing well?
This simple switch in focus can open your thinking to a whole raft of positive aspects of a situation.

Switching your focus helps raise your awareness of what, when and where you are placing your energy. The good news is that this focus is not fixed — it can be changed at any time.

> Do you lead a group or team?
> If you do, try to switch your focus to the people who are not being heard rather than the loudest ones.

Switching your focus starts with a pause. What, where and who am I focusing on at this moment? This can be enlightening. You could, for example, be ignoring something (or someone) that might be vital to understanding a situation or solving a problem.

For example, you can switch your starting point.

Let's imagine you are the owner of a restaurant and diners are complaining about how long it takes for the meals to arrive.

The usual starting point might be to investigate the workflow in the kitchen, the efficiency of the serving staff, and so on.

Pause.

Switch to a different starting point: the diners' sense of time. Perhaps you can indicate on the menu how long each meal might take to arrive or strategically place some mirrors around the restaurant so diners can see themselves, which might encourage them to adjust their appearance rather than only focusing on waiting times.

The lesson?

You do not have to always start where you always have started. Your focus is more dynamic and changeable than you realise.

Switch to mental health

One of the most important and far-reaching examples of switching your focus is the shift from physical health to mental health. Historically, in the sporting arena, players and coaches would focus on fitness, strength, flexibility, diet, and so on.

In the education field, the emphasis was on such things as marks, attendance and in-class contribution. In organisational life, leaders focused on results, budgets, returns on investments, and so on.

This was a Box Mode focus: measurable, objective and rational.

Yet something was missing.

They were focusing on only part of the person.

Then a wonderful shift occurred: they started to focus more on mental health. This was more of a Ball Mode focus. As shown in figure 8.2, you can switch your focus from physical to mental health and back again at any time.

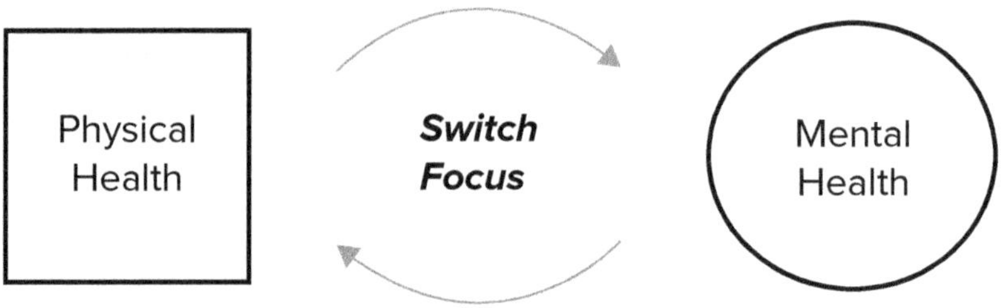

Figure 8.2 Switching between physical and mental health

The focus on mental health introduced new metrics such as stress levels, burnout risk, resilience, anxiety and depression, and emotional energy.

Leaders, parents and coaches started asking new questions such as:

- How are you really doing?
- Is this person thriving or just surviving?
- How can we build psychological safety?

And these weren't just individual reflections.

Organisations, schools and sporting teams started building mental health into their systems. It expanded who was responsible and how to address this.

Previously, health was viewed as an individual duty: your responsibility, your discipline, your self-care.

But switching focus to mental health distributed responsibility:

- Employers began offering mental health days, coaching and employee assistance programs.

- Teachers started checking in on student wellbeing, not just academic performance.
- Coaches and sports clubs embedded mental skills training into regular routines.

Now, the system itself, not just the person, is expected to support mental health. This switch to a greater awareness of mental health also raised awareness of short-term and longer-term performance, health and resilience.

In elite sport, there has been a noticeable shift to sports psychology as the new focus of performance. This has resulted in a new language, measurements and preparation such as visualisation techniques, breathing and focus drills, emotional regulation and mindset coaching.

The lesson?

A simple, yet significant switch in focus opened an entirely new way of operating, educating, coaching, teaching, performing and leading!

It's Box *and* Ball Mode focus

When you switch your focus, you don't just change what you see — you change what's possible.

Being able to switch your focus is more than a tool. It's a creative shift. What you focus on shapes how you think, feel and act. And with a simple switch you can transform how you engage with the world.

It's more than switching your perspective. While this is a wonderful first step, when you switch your focus, you can unlock a new understanding and a rich array of possibilities. You are trying to connect and elevate different (often unseen) areas of focus.

Here's another example.

Imagine you're watching a presentation.

A Box Mode focus: The facts, slides and talking points

Switch.

A Ball Mode focus: The emotion, energy and body language.

It's what's said and how it's said.

A presentation without facts, data or results lacks credibility. Yet one without a story is boring and lacks engagement. When you combine Box Mode focus with Ball Mode focus, you can see more of the total landscape.

Team leaders often focus on behaviours and results. This makes sense: it's explicit and observable. But an equally valuable focus is on values, principles, relationships or attitudes. The so-called softer side of leadership is often the most difficult.

Part of the reason is that in Box Mode much of what is intangible is simply not seen. And because of this it is not deemed important. This is why being aware of your (and others') focus is so empowering and insightful.

Pause.

Now switch by asking new questions:

- What am I missing?
- What am I or we not seeing?
- What are others seeing that I cannot?

Play: Select one of these questions that interests you and play with it for a few minutes. What emerges?

How to use with AI

AI follows your focus.

So, whatever you focus on, AI will do the same but can emphasise it. This is why switching your focus can be so powerful with AI.

Humans provide the direction with their prompts and AI amplifies it. Much like a telescope can amplify the human eye but the human still controls what is being investigated.

For example, you can ask AI to:

Switch off: Facts.
Switch on: Meaning (i.e. ask for patterns, insights or connections rather than raw data).
Switch off: Watching what everyone else is doing.
Switch on: Feeling what the customer experiences.

This switch in focus might also help you overcome any bias or assumptions you might have made. All you need is an openness to switching your focus on something you usually don't and see what happens.

You can also ask AI to select a different focus in any situation. For example, when you are trying to understand why a team you lead is not quite firing on all cylinders, you might ask AI to focus on values, relationships, energy levels, age, generational influences, diversity, personalities or meeting places.

Or, ask AI to prompt you with *We are focused on the results; now, let's switch and focus on the skills of the team.*

I love helping people switch their focus. It's simple, easy and reversible (i.e. you can switch back to your usual focus). And in a world that is focused (it seems) entirely on what divides us it is an empowering thought that this is not fixed. You can switch and focus on what we all have in common.

2-minute Switch Thinking exercise

What are you focused on?

At your next presentation try to switch your focus for a few minutes. It could be on your:

- voice, dress
- words
- body language
- energy levels, confidence.

What do you notice? What can you enhance for your next presentation?

Chapter 9

Switch on your imagination

I recently went channel surfing, and decided to download the latest *Superman* movie — and it's a hoot. But to totally enjoy the movie I needed to switch my thinking from Box Mode to Ball Mode. By doing so, I allowed my imagination to wander and roll with the thrills, spills and adventure of Superman saving the world (again!).

My imagination switches on when I go to art galleries and venture bravely into the modern art section. I am often surprised, amazed, shocked and challenged by contemporary art.

Now I want you to imagine the biggest switch of all.

Imagine being able to switch on your imagination, anytime, anywhere. You don't have to wait for a movie, art gallery or brainstorming session. And you don't have to wait for inspiration or to be in the right mood.

How amazing would that be!

Is it even possible?

Well …

As kids, we played with monsters in the bath, built forts from pillows, flew to space with cardboard boxes and fought pirates at the beach.

Imagination was the default — not the exception.

Imagine you're a bird flying over your city. What do you see? Where would you go?

Then something happened: we grew up, got serious and swapped pretend play for real problems. But your imagination didn't vanish. It just got quiet, or to use a technology phrase, we put our imagination in 'sleep mode'.

And that is a great pity because we all need our individual and collective imagination more than ever.

Just think about your imagination for a moment.

It's free, universal and unlimited. And it can be accessed by individuals, groups and teams. You cannot run out of this amazing resource. What's more, it's a distinctly human capability (take that AI!).

But most of us have paradoxically forgotten about it. Or at least we do not know how to access it.

Why?

Our education system often trains us to be right, not original. Then, when we enter the workforce, a premium is placed on formal, planned, controlled progress rather than potentially risky leaps of imagination.

We start to live in Box Mode.

What's worse, many of us are told we are not creative. In the advertising world, for example, there is the creative department and there are other departments (presumably the non-creatives).

What a waste of human potential just when we need it more than ever to tackle issues like kids' obesity, an epidemic of anxiety, a decline in trust — not to mention climate change.

A new understanding of imagination

For too long, imagination has been treated like a divine force: rare, mystical and unreachable. It was the providence of a few remarkable individuals. We now know that imagination is within all of us. And it's located (brain scientists believe) in our DMN (which, as you know, I call Ball Mode).

This is a profound shift.

It means that rather than just looking outwards for inspiration we can also look inwards. We can all imagine. It's built into the architecture of our brain.

The great news is that when you switch your thinking to Ball Mode, you can turn your imagination back on.

> A friend of mine has set up a weekend business buying and selling old vinyl records at the local market. He loves it. If you had to develop a new money-making gig on the weekends, what would it be?
>
> Congratulations! You are using your imagination.

And now, more than ever, if it can be imagined, it can be built. Who would have imagined that cash is almost a thing of the past? That robots could be doing operations on humans and driverless cars might replace human-driven cars within 10 years?

But here we are.

What was once imagined is now a reality.

Athletes have known about using their imagination to improve their performance for years. They visualise themselves competing in a race. In their mind's eye, they can see themselves warming up, feeling confident, exploding from the blocks and running each step. They can even see the finish line — all in their imagination.

When I was doing my PhD, I used to visualise my graduation ceremony, being dressed in my gown, looking out at my family who were all smiles.

This image helped me to keep plugging away when times were tough. My imagination helped me to connect the current, with the future; my everyday work on my thesis and research, with my end goal.

Switching on your imagination is not only beneficial in reaching some future goal but it can also boost your mood, optimism and general wellbeing right now. It only takes a few minutes each day.

For example, in the next 2 minutes:

Switch off: What might go wrong, what you lack or what you should have done.

Switch on: In your mind's eye, see yourself receiving an award, getting promoted or graduating from university.

How to switch on your imagination — right now!

Most of the time we live in the world of *what is.*

We often ask ourselves *what is* the situation, problem or challenge? Through necessity, we live in the present and in the box of our grounded reality. It's structured, necessary and efficient.

We deal with facts, figures, deadlines and decisions. We often work in teams, navigate tasks and focus on what is in front of us. We have our ever-expanding to-do list, limited time and budgets as we try to get through the day as best as we can.

But what if we could switch to a different, more imaginative world?

The world of *what could be.*

It's a world of future possibilities, play and many surprises. One that is unbounded, optimistic and energising. Look at figure 9.1 and imagine the switch from the 'what is' world to the 'what could be' one (remember you can always switch back).

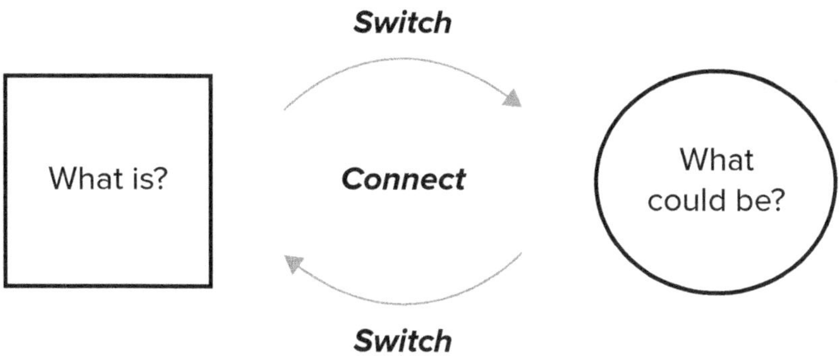

Figure 9.1 Switching between 'what is' and 'what could be'

To enter the world of *what could be*, you could go for a walk, have a long shower or visit a bookstore. This can trigger your DMN and fire up your imagination. Though whether your DMN kicks in is often a random occurrence.

Why leave this precious resource to chance? Why not access it when you need it, anywhere, anytime. To do this, you need to switch on your imagination by using a range of prompts.

In a world of information overload, you need your imagination more than ever. Your team might be stuck and rather than hope for inspiration to strike, you pause and ask, 'If we were a startup with limited funds how might we solve this problem?' Suddenly you have changed your group's thinking from business-as-usual solutions to some disruptive ones. This one switch might just open a new wave of possibilities.

To give you a real-life example, it was only a few years ago that the idea of curing cancer was a pipedream. But someone, somewhere needed the courage to imagine the seemingly impossible. And while curing all cancers is a long way off, in Australia, the human papillomavirus vaccine introduced in 2007 has almost eliminated cervical cancer. Indeed, in 2021 no cervical cancer cases were reported in women under 25!

To imagine is to start work towards creating a better future.

Here are some imagination prompts you can use by yourself, with others and with AI:

- *I wonder…*
  I use this all the time.

  'I wonder' is gentle, open-ended and non-judgemental, inviting playful exploration rather than demanding answers. Even the language suggests being transported to some magical place. For example, I wonder what the world would look like if politicians were paid only based on how they improved both the economy and society.

  'I wonder' is personal, emotional and often tied to curiosity, longing or hope. It's classic Ball Mode. And yet it can be provocative and disruptive.

  The other big advantage is that it works beautifully with AI. 'I wonder' prompts wide-ranging, creative output while allowing for unexpected connections (i.e. used as an imaginative prompt).

  Example: 'I wonder what cities might look like if every building could breathe'. This might lead you (and others) to think more about living gardens on every building or creating more space for wildlife and humans to live side by side.

- *What if …*
  This is another simple and powerful way to switch to Ball Mode and access your DMN. It invites alternate realities and scenario-building—core functions of imagination and future simulation.

'What if' immediately creates space between current constraints and imagined possibility.

When used with AI, it forms a creative conversation. There is no good or bad, right or wrong—just 'what if'. It's perfect when used as an imaginative prompt.

Prompt engineering example: 'How could we improve our public transport system?'
Prompt imagining example: 'What if kids designed the next public transport system? What might they suggest?'
This might lead to a drastic change in the transport system around schools.
'What if' is a fast, easy and imaginative switch to boost exploration, ideation or future thinking.

- *I've been dreaming of ...*
  I love the intimacy of this. It reminds me of Dr Martin Luther King's 'I have a dream' speech. It taps straight into your memory, emotion, longing and purpose. It's your dream, not anyone else's.

  'I've been dreaming of' takes you from the present to the future, from limitations to possibility with one tiny switch. A desired state seems more within reach.

  Example: 'I've been dreaming of a university where students swap roles with professors, once per week'.

  Used with AI, it provides direction and depth, allowing AI to enhance and shape a vision.

  Example: An imaginative AI prompt could be: 'I've been dreaming of a neighbourhood that cares more for the lonely. Can you give me five ways to make this happen?'

- *'Imagine if ...'*
  Don't you love the sound of this? 'Imagine if all your team members worked together for the greater good'. It's bold, visual and direct.

  I love the optimism in this prompt. When you use the expression 'imagine if' anything is possible.

  Example: 'Imagine if every team leader or boss had "kindness" as one of their key performance indicators'.

  And this is where AI can help you the most. It does not judge or evaluate instantly; it does not cross its arms or have a disapproving frown. If you can create an 'Imagine if', then AI can get to work.

  Example using AI: Imagine if everyone in the organisation had a Help KPI (i.e. to try and help someone else, every day). How could your team make this happen?

  ChatGPT instantly came up with a few suggestions:
  - Start talking about it.
  - Celebrate any small wins.
  - Have a help wall ...

  Suddenly this imaginative prompt (i.e. 'a Help KPI') came to life.
- *Let's pretend ...*
  This prompt takes you back to your childhood. When you pretend, you bypass logic and ego. You do not worry about right or wrong.

  'Let's pretend' also reawakens childhood play — you are in your sandpit imagining new possibilities and connections.

Example: 'Let's pretend your pet could speak — what would it say to you?'

When you use this prompt with other humans and AI it encourages unexpected — even humorous — directions and conversations that can lead to real breakthroughs.

- *In the future…*
  This prompt helps you tap into your mental time travel. 'In the future' anything is possible. This is an ideal prompt if you want to escape the current ideas and solutions. It is also non-threatening because who knows what will happen in the future?

  'In the future' is a powerful way to move from small changes to gigantic leaps.

  Example: 'In the future, what is the role of teachers when most learning could happen by students interacting with AI?' (Although I have noticed that Sweden is returning to physical books, handwriting and paper based learning.)

Being able to switch on your imagination is empowering and energising. It's a wonderful feeling to play in Ball Mode. You can just imagine without always having an outcome in mind.

Your imagination is distinctly yours. It's a safe place, a sanctuary and a sand pit of fun, play and possibilities. And it's instant. You can transport yourself to another world, time or place in a moment!

Switch on your imagination is also wonderful for teams. Just imagine if you could unleash the full creative potential of a group of people. Any of these prompts can be used by the team or perhaps you can encourage each team member to use the prompt they prefer on the next challenge and then come together and discuss what ideas have been generated.

The situation: The group has hit a brick wall.

Switch off: Group discussion.

Switch on: Individual imagining for 2 minutes (e.g. in the future), then discussing with others.

As I am writing this, I am imagining my wake (it's a bit weird, I know). My family and friends are remembering me with laughter and affection. I am hovering with a smile on my face. What does this all mean? Who knows, but this image came to me and it makes me feel loved.

What is exciting is that your imagination has not gone away. You can rekindle it easily and quickly by switching to Ball Mode and hence your DMN.

This is a key point. Switch Thinking is built around 2-minute switches and a switch off and switch on process. So why not a 2-minute burst of imagination? Go for it, play and see where your imagination takes you.

For example, your primary-aged school kids won't go to bed on time and rather than get agitated you say, 'Who would like to hear a story about Sammy the Scaredy Shark?' The next night, 'Who would like to hear about Tommy the Timid Tiger?' Using your imagination in this way is fun, engaging and you might discover a new confidence in your creativity that you can use every day.

I find that AI gives me greater confidence to use my imagination even more. By doing so I can greatly enhance my creativity, problem solving and decision making. And because I know that I can return to Box Mode at any time I find myself taking more risks with my thinking.

For example, I asked AI to connect two things I love to do (yoga and visiting an art gallery) to create a potential new business idea.

AI came up with Stillness and Story: pop-up yoga classes inside art galleries, blending movement, mindfulness and imagination. How cool is that!

I love the idea of human imagination driven by AI.

> Imagine you could talk to a historical figure you admire (perhaps Mahatma Gandhi, Marie Curie or Jane Austen, to name a few).
>
> What would you ask them?
>
> With your imagination (and perhaps the help of AI) this is possible.

The interaction between Box Mode and Ball Mode

Imagination can help you soar. However, even a majestic eagle needs to land to rest, eat and care for their young. Switching back to Box Mode can help you ground your imagination.

> What does your life look like in 3 years' time? Are you excited by what you see? Let go of logic for the next 2 minutes. Play with possibility. Are you married? Living overseas? Studying?
>
> Now return to the present. Switch back to Box Mode. What is one action you can start doing right now to manifest your future success?

It's the dynamic interaction between 'what is' and 'what could be' that often leads to a breakthrough.

2-minute Switch Thinking exercise

I wonder...

I find the easiest imagination prompt to use is 'I wonder'. It's gentle, non-judgemental and playful. I am writing this in a café and I wonder what would happen if everyone in the café was encouraged to wear a name tag (perhaps they would get a free coffee).

The name tag might encourage people to say 'hi' to one another.

It could be nothing more.

I wonder...

When I use this expression, I find my mind drifting off. I can imagine a friendlier buzz at the café.

Just start using it; let it drift into your conversation. Allow yourself some time and space to see what your mind and those of others might come up with when they start wondering.

It's a lovely way to give your curiosity some tangible form.

Chapter 10

Switch your emotion

A few years ago, I worked with the leaders of a management consulting firm. Their challenge was 'How do we attract the best and brightest graduates to our firm?'

I let the group discuss this challenge for a while, then I paused and suggested that we switch the challenge by using emotional language.

Blank looks ensued. I persevered. Emotions such as joy, frustration and anger, I suggested. Eventually one of the younger consultants suggested the following as a new problem statement:

'How do we become the most loved brand in the country?'

This led to a stunned silence, then the room exploded with ideas and energy.

The insight?

They realised that if their firm became the most loved brand in the country, then graduates would flock to it.

'Who might we now compete with?' they asked. Not other consulting companies, but companies like Nike or LEGO. 'How to measure this new ambition' was another question they asked themselves.

From incremental, boring ideas and solutions, a simple switch to emotional language sparked a completely new level of creativity, insight and understanding. The consultants saw this problem differently.

The message?

You have more control over your emotions than you realise.

Picture the volume control on your smartphone, tablet, laptop or speakers. You can increase or decrease the volume depending on the situation. The volume of your favourite music might be quite different at a party as opposed when you're cramming for an exam (or maybe not!).

Now imagine the music is your emotion. And you have a volume control where you can switch up your emotion or switch it down depending on the situation. Much like a dimmer switch in a light.

The key point is this: you can be more in control of your emotions by switching your thinking. You can turn the volume up when you are trying to energise yourself or a team (Ball Mode) and then turn it down if the conversation gets personal (Box Mode). This idea of turning your emotion up or down is illustrated in figure 10.1.

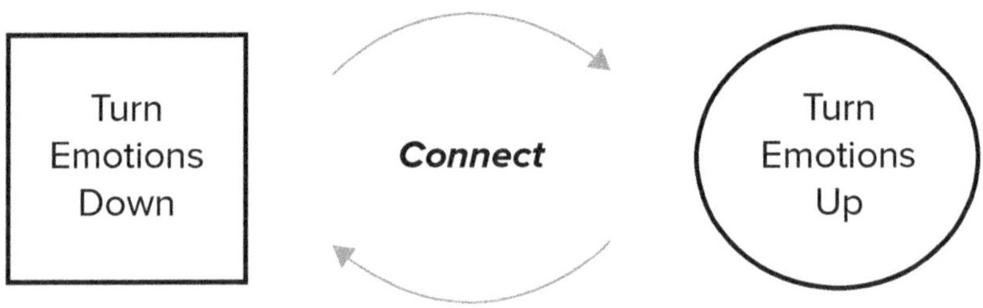

Figure 10.1 Switching your emotion up or down

> Think about your last presentation. How emotive was it from, say, 1 to 10? How can you make your next one more engaging and inspiring?

The power of turning up emotions

I was taught in my corporate life and at MBA school that I should not show my emotions at work—to do so was to show weakness, it could mean that I was out of control.

How wrong I was.

Emotions, I have since learned through my Switch Thinking workshops, are vital in almost everything—from problem solving to decision making. They are also the bridge to your DMN and its role in releasing your imagination and creativity.

Think of the world's great brands. Apple, for example, may not be as innovative as in the Steve Jobs era but the experience of using their products is still magical and all their products and packaging are quite beautiful. Volvo is a prestige car, but its real appeal is safety.

Pure emotion.

Switch off: Thinking of what could go wrong

Switch on: A scenario where a difficult conversation goes much better than you expect. What does it feel like?

We tend to buy on emotions and justify with our reason. Concepts such as brand loyalty are an emotional concept. Patagonia, for example, offer wonderful products but invite their customers to be part of a cause. The emotional appeal is brand identification and contribution.

Here is another example.

The most engaging presentations are often exercises in storytelling supported by facts. When we interview someone, we are often asking ourselves, 'Can I trust this person? Would they have my back? Would they be fun to work with?'

And yet…

Many leaders in the corporate arena, in my experience, have trouble even acknowledging they or others have emotions, and if they do, they have trouble talking about these. Perhaps a new generation of leaders will be better equipped, with greater awareness of concepts such as EI (emotional intelligence).

> Do you have a new idea for a podcast based on something you love? How might you attract other people who love the same thing?

I well remember the senior leader of a bank complaining to me that a particular group in a brainstorming session that I was facilitating was having too much fun. I had to reassure him that the fun they were displaying was essential for generating and bouncing ideas off one another. Sure enough, this group produced the best solutions on the day.

This is no surprise. The brain research suggests that emotion fuels motivation, connection, memory and action. Switching to Ball Mode and hence your DMN is where empathy, storytelling and self-awareness live. All it takes is a small switch of emotion.

For example:

From: What if I don't get the job?
Switch to: What a great adventure, no matter the outcome.

It's reason *and* emotion

The language of business is rational. The problem I have found with this starting point is that problems defined in rational terms (i.e. Box Mode) often produce rational, safe and incremental ideas.

A better approach is to frame challenges in both rational and emotional terms.

What people in my workshops seem to love about the Switch Thinking approach is that you can still feel safe with the tried-and-true rational Box Mode thinking and then explore new possibilities for just a few minutes with a more emotional Ball Mode approach. Then switch back or connect the two modes, as illustrated in figure 10.2.

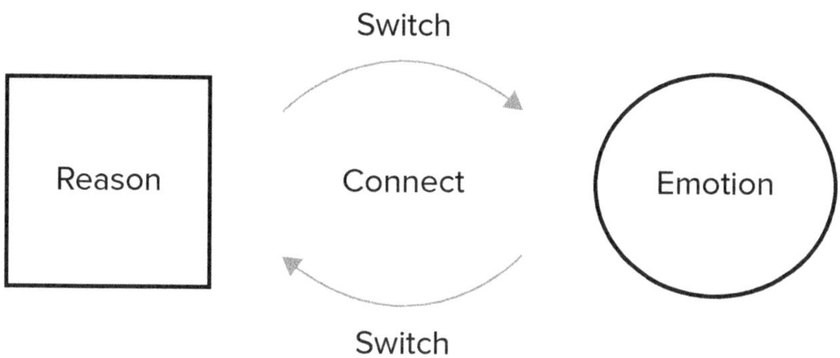

Figure 10.2 Switching between reason and emotion

This switching back and forth provides safety and some risk. The usual with the different. The predictable with the surprising.

Exploring a range of emotions doesn't have to feel overwhelming—it can be brief, playful and revealing. When you switch up your emotions even just for 2 minutes it can lead to a deeper understanding and openness.

You might say, 'I know this is a group decision, but I am feeling uneasy about what we are proposing. Can we discuss a different option for a few minutes?'

This type of switching with time limits gives you and others permission to explore new possibilities without judgement.

Switch your emotions to create, change and grow

Many workplaces today are emotionally squeezed. They are high-pressure, structured and you need to perform or move on. This creates stress, fear of failure and pressure to conform, and yet leaders rarely talk about it.

Switching to emotions at an individual and collective level offers a release valve — a way to talk about emotions in a safe, structured way.

For example:

- What are the facts?
  Switch.
  How are people feeling?
- How are the sales going?
  Switch.
  How are the relationships?

This switching approach can give you permission to lead emotionally. Switch Thinking opens the door for team leaders to say, 'Let's switch gears — what are we feeling right now?'

Switching to emotion also places purpose, values and belonging on centre stage. Younger employees in particular care increasingly about having an emotional connection to their work or at least to have what they do aligned with their values.

Team exercise

What are our behaviours?

Switch.

What are our values?

Are these aligned?

Being able to switch back and forth between Box Mode and Ball Mode means rational planning, controls and delivery can live side by side with emotional insight.

Paradoxically, using AI is a helpful vehicle for expressing your emotions.

For example:

> *Prompt:* AI, I am feeling nervous about presenting these ideas. Can you find other examples of where this type of solution may have worked in a different industry or situation?

AI can become your trusted creative and emotional partner and collaborator. It's personal, unique to you and extremely fast. And it can keep your confidence!

To use an analogy, switching your emotions up is like jumping into the surf and you experience that cold shiver down your spine. Then you get used to it and often have the time of your life surfing the waves as they come in.

> Are you facing a decision you've been putting off?
>
> What is the risk-free option?
>
> *Switch.*
>
> In the next 2 minutes explore a left-field option. How do you feel?

Using Switch Thinking with someone who is emotional

In my experience working with leaders, coaches and facilitators, one of the most difficult challenges is to try and connect with someone who is upset, defensive or angry.

The usual response is to stay in Box Mode and perhaps explain, correct, offer solutions or ask them to calm down. This is understandable but rarely works (in my experience) because the emotional person does not feel heard.

Here is a three-step approach I use:

1. *Switch yourself first.*
   In these moments, I try and switch to Ball Mode so that I can connect with the other person on an emotional level. You remain calm, yet curious. The goal is empathy without judgement (Box Mode, by comparison, is designed for reason, detachment and evaluation). In this step you are not challenging the other person's emotion. They, in a sense, have a right to feel how they wish. I try to build connection so together we can design a potential way forward.
2. *Name and mirror the emotion.*
   In this step you try to build safety and respect (e.g. 'It sounds like you are really frustrated ... '). The goal here is to acknowledge how they are feeling and try to understand their view of a situation. This is validating and respectful.
3. *Invite a switch to Box Mode.*
   Once I have a sense that the emotional heat has cooled, I try to suggest a way forward (e.g. 'Could we work on a few options together?' or 'How can I help you right now, in the next 2 minutes?). I like this step in particular because you have met them emotionally first, then you are giving them agency over how to proceed.

Using random emotion

If you are in a brainstorming or problem-solving session or just need a new idea, try selecting an emotion at random. It does not matter what emotion you choose — you are just trying to escape the status quo.

It could be fear. What are we really scared of? What might happen if we were all fearless?

Or anger.

What's really annoying our customers? How could we turn this around, so they love us?

Or nostalgia.

What's something from our childhood that we could bring back (e.g. vinyl records)?

Or curiosity.

What's a question that we have not asked yet?

Then play with this emotion to develop some new ideas in the next 2 minutes (AI can kick in here to help).

For example, say you were having trouble with a neighbour on the floor above you. You could use the Pause — Switch — Play cycle.

Pause.

Switch to a random emotion: joy.

Now play with this emotion.

My mind instantly goes to how I could bring more joy to my neighbour's life. Perhaps as a starting point, find out what their interests are or the sports they watch. Then bring this up when you next have a conversation with them.

This may be a bit of a stretch, but suddenly you are feeling joyful rather than resentful towards your neighbour. You could even bring in your neighbour's garbage bin, for example, as a kind-hearted gesture.

Try drawing the solution

Sometimes you can access your emotions and hence access your default mode network by drawing a solution to the problem at hand.

This is a simple but powerful switch from words to pictures.

In my workshops I often start by asking participants to draw in 60 seconds (so it does not become a drawing competition) how they are feeling right now and what they would like to feel at the end of the workshop.

These drawings are fun, insightful and often evocative. They are also unleashing their emotions without me explicitly saying 'switch on your emotions'.

It's the food!

Some years ago, I was asked by a major airline leadership team to help develop a better passenger experience. For six months, I worked with the various flight crews to help them achieve this goal.

I asked the flight crew (in groups of 20) to work by themselves and to draw what frustrates the passengers the most. Notice the framing of this challenge: 'What frustrates passengers the most?' This emotional language is a way to switch to Ball Mode to draw this image (hence accessing your DMN).

The pictures were revealing. In well over 50 per cent of cases there was a picture of the food being served. This made perfect sense from the flight crew's perspective as they were held responsible for the type, choice and quality of food during the flight.

I talked eagerly about what I had found with the leadership team. They initially rejected the findings. In frustration, I took 20 of the hand-drawn pictures up to the leadership team and went through them one by one.

Finally, there was an 'aha' moment with one of the leaders saying, 'It's the food'. Yes, I said. One way to improve the in-flight passenger experience was to improve your food, I explained. Six months later I flew on this airline and to my delight the quality of the food had dramatically improved.

The key message of this example was that if you ask Box Mode questions, you often only receive Box-Mode-like answers (e.g. 'Are you satisfied with the food? Please rate it on a 7-point scale'. Asking front-line staff for their feedback using Ball Mode emotional techniques and by drawing images can often uncover powerful new insights.

Switching your emotion also has another benefit. At work we often evaluate our new ideas or solutions using some form of rational point-scoring system. I have found that this approach is useful in Box Mode thinking. But it often lacks passion for the idea. Without passion and energy, even the high-scoring ideas are often not tested. Many people will say to me, 'Yes, we must do this', but they have no energy to execute the idea.

To evaluate any idea, solution or opportunity you need to score both Box Mode issues (e.g. 'Do we have the necessary resources?') and Ball Mode questions (e.g. 'Are we proud of this idea?').

Switch what you feel, think and do

Switching how you feel (either up or down) can also change your thinking and hence what you do. Think about this as an interconnected system. It does not matter where you start — the moment you switch one, you switch the others as well.

For example, when I am lacking motivation, I often open YouTube and click on a video of, say, a flashmob playing Beethoven's 'Ode to Joy'. Look it up as it still brings tears to my eyes and instantly, I feel more inspired.

Switch down your emotion

Of course, switching works both ways. While much of this chapter has discussed the many benefits of switching up your emotion (Ball Mode) you also need to be able to switch it down when you need to

(Box Mode). This might be to regain clarity, perspective or calm. And to encourage analysis, detachment and structure.

I am sure everyone has experienced this situation. You're about to fire off an angry email or text. But then you pause and think: perhaps it's better that I send this tomorrow after a good night's sleep.

This is switching down your emotion. By pausing you might have just saved yourself from doing something that you might regret later.

AI can help you here.

For example:

- What would a calm version of me do right now?
- How might a Buddhist monk react in this situation?
- What would I say to someone else feeling this way?

This is a key point. You have more control over your emotions than you realise. Often, it's a case of pausing and asking yourself, 'How am I feeling? Is this in line with the moment? And how are others feeling? Am I in sync with them?'

Then ask yourself, 'Do I need to switch up or switch down my emotion?'

You can switch.

You have agency.

You are not imprisoned by your emotions — in fact, they can set you free!

2-minute Switch Thinking exercise

The message?

Ask yourself, 'How am I feeling right now?'

Frustrated because it's raining and I could not play golf.

Switch to another feeling for a few minutes.

Select 'appreciation'. Why? Completely random.

Trust it. Stay with it for the next 2 minutes.

What happens? How do you feel now?

Sometimes just naming how you feel right now is insightful. You don't have to understand why. I have found that when you ask people how they feel (in work situations, in particular) they might say 'bored'. When they have expressed this emotion, it is like a balloon, where all the air rushes out. Once they do this, most people can then move on as they can't keep saying 'I am bored' (most adults anyway).

Now switch to another feeling for 2 minutes. It does not matter which one.

It's a small switch that may have a big impact.

Chapter 11

Switch your rules

Think of any formal game you have played in your life. Let's take golf, for example. The R&A (i.e. the Royal and Ancient Golf Club of St Andrews) developed and administered the official rules of golf. These are the explicit rules that all golfers abide by.

Then there are unofficial rules or golf etiquette that can help the game move along and show respect for other players (e.g. park your buggy to the side of the green, not in front of it). There are also local rules for each individual club that take into consideration the state of the course, out of bound areas, neighbourhood considerations, and so on.

There are numerous advantages in having a set of official and unofficial rules. It means that any golfer knows what is acceptable and what is not. These rules can be the last word on any golfing arguments or disputes. It means that I can play on any course knowing that if I follow these rules, I can enjoy the game and not be penalised.

These rules are clear, transparent and shared among all players.

Your thinking rules

Just like there are rules of golf, there are also thinking rules. They are not written down, yet they are real. Your rules are your assumptions, beliefs, conventions, past experiences and theories you use that build a relatively stable neural pattern. These are important because they are efficient, have worked before and you have become comfortable following them. Over time, however, as you use these rules again and again, they can become rigid rather than adaptable. They guide but can also limit your thinking — sometimes consciously, other times unconsciously.

These rules inform what you see, think, feel, expect and do. For example, you expect the lawyers and partners in a law firm to dress and speak in a particular way. There is no explicit rule that says they must — it's what you expect and the conventions that all the firms tend to follow in the law industry.

By contrast, think of all the rules of work that have been challenged and broken in the past few years. You might not have to go into an office five days a week, nor work from 9 to 5 or dress in a formal way, to name just a few historical traditions that have recently been overturned.

And for the most part this is entirely liberating. In fact, I am writing this chapter not in an office but in a café surrounded by a diverse range of people having a rich array of conversations.

There are also team or group rules. These might include unspoken norms (e.g. We don't challenge the boss), certain roles (e.g. Julie is the 'ideas' person; Alex does the planning), cultural codes (e.g. in this team, we don't talk about emotion) and legacy assumptions (e.g. we can't suggest a premium product because it didn't work five years ago).

These collective rules can restrict teams just as powerfully as beliefs can limit individuals. And because they're shared, they can be harder to spot but even more powerful to switch. A team's collective rules can subtly reinforce each other until one person has the courage to challenge a rule.

In addition, in group settings there are often physical or environmental rules. These might include, for example, where people sit in meetings or who speaks first, or which rooms or tools get used for 'serious' vs 'creative' work.

It is why, for example, switching the physical environment (e.g. taking a meeting outside) can sometimes break the thinking rules, which in turn can open minds to new possibilities.

In most situations there are no right or wrong rules. Just the rules that you tend to follow in most circumstances. What's also interesting is that your thinking rules may be completely different from mine. Why? Because you have a whole set of different experiences, assumptions and expectations than I do. Once you realise this, you can better understand why two people can experience something yet have completely different recollections.

In the next 2 minutes write down what your thinking rules are around a challenge that you are facing right now.

I have assumed that...

I believe...

I tend to follow this convention...

This is what I have always done...

Your thinking rules are often efficient but can blind you to new possibilities. They may have worked before and can provide short-cuts in thinking. But in a changing world where new competitors may not follow the same set of rules they can leave you feeling vulnerable.

Here are some examples of brands or organisations breaking the so-called rules:

- The Singapore Zoo broke the rule that zoos had to be open only during the day by introducing a night safari.
- Swatch broke the rule that you should only have one watch.
- IKEA broke the rule that furniture was sold ready to use by introducing flat-packs and asking consumers to assemble it (sometimes to my frustration).

Breaking the formal or informal rules can also be applied to individuals.

For example:

- Dr Jane Goodall broke the rule that animals are passive subjects to be observed at a distance with a deep, empathetic connection with individual chimpanzees.
- Greta Thunberg broke the rule that young people aren't taken seriously in politics by becoming a global speaker on the environment.
- Taylor Swift broke the rule that artists must stick to one genre by leaping from country to pop music.
- Simone Biles broke the rule that athletes should endure pressure at all costs by prioritising her mental wellbeing over competition.

Notice with all these examples how breaking the old rules is now well established, yet at the time these rule-breakers required courage and imagination.

> Remember a time in your life where you broke the rules (e.g. assumption, belief, convention). What happened? What did you learn?

I have used the word 'rules' as a provocative way to categorise a set of explicit and implicit patterns that inform your thinking and hence how you feel and what you do. Indeed, for some people in my workshops the idea that you can challenge or change these rules is a revelation.

Following the road rules is obviously a great idea. But your thinking is different. You can switch or change your rules at any time. My younger daughter started an interview by asking a potential employer a range of questions. She was interviewing them. This is a switch of the usual rules but so impressed the leader that she offered her a job on the spot! If you don't challenge your own and others' rules, your thinking can become rigid and you end up being stuck in your own thinking box.

For example, you can think in twos (e.g. right – wrong, pass – fail).

Switch.

You can think in threes (e.g. a usual response, a different one and a radical one).

Thinking in threes can open up your mind to new possibilities — and all you did was slightly change your thinking rules.

The key point here is that many of the thinking rules that we follow (unlike the golf rules) can be changed. They can be challenged, updated and thrown out.

You can switch them.

> Every time you observe a thinking rule (e.g. assumption, belief, etc.), try to make it explicit (e.g. 'Our assumption is that our competitors will keep doing the same things as last year. Is this still valid? What might they do that could surprise us?')

So, what is stopping you from switching your thinking rules? Partly it's that you don't realise that these rules are limiting and partly it's the idea that you can change them. They are not set in stone.

Think of the historical rules around retirement. You work until your retirement age, then play bowls, move to the coast or a retirement village and see out your days. This may suit some people, but boomers are redefining what it means to retire. The idea of retiring from life seems a completely outdated idea. Picasso, for example, was still painting in his 80s — in fact, right up to 91 years. We don't all have to be like Picasso, but we can reject the old rules of retirement and paint a full life of, say, writing, volunteering, travelling and mentoring.

These rules are typically expressed in Box Mode. In fact, a box is the perfect metaphor for your thinking rules.

Let's consider a challenge: how to make meetings more engaging. Draw a box. Now list your assumptions, beliefs, experiences and expectations around this challenge. For example, 'Everyone in the team should stay for the whole meeting'. These thinking rules can be captured in a box (see figure 11.1).

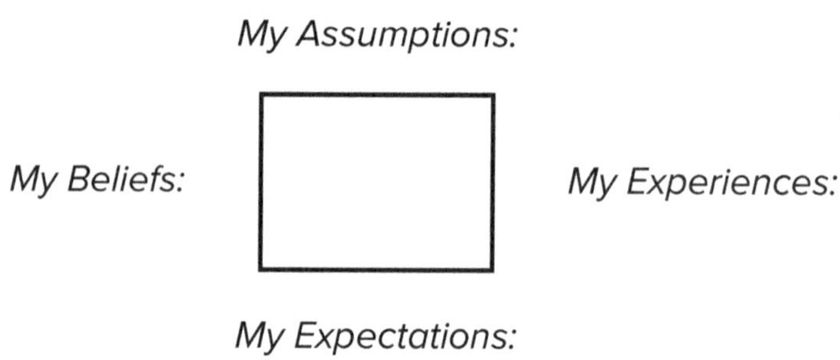

Figure 11.1 Your mindset box

Note that it forms a box that can trap you as the sides become more and more rigid. To break free of your thinking box, try switching some or all of your thinking rules (e.g. 'Team members need only attend the parts of a meeting that are relevant to them').

Can you see that how you think is dictated by the rules you follow?

Any problem or challenge also comes with its own set of rules. For example, I worked in advertising for a while, and I mentioned to a client that they did not have an advertising problem but rather they had a distribution challenge. You simply could not access their product at the right time, I suggested. The client thanked me but ignored my advice. Their mind was limited to finding an advertising solution.

The first step in switching your thinking rules is to see and understand the rules you're obeying.

Next, I'm going to present my insight after working with hundreds of leadership teams over the past 20 years.

Make the rules explicit

Rules shape not just what you do, but how you think, feel and relate to others. I have found that when you make these rules visible, you can reshape your world.

When you take these thinking rules out into the open, they can be discussed, challenged and, if necessary, overturned. These rules are not good or bad, they are just limiting.

In fact, some of the rules may still be relevant.

Numerous times I have been in workshops after I have explained the limiting impact of thinking rules and participants have said something like, 'I have always assumed we had to sell this product for under $20'. On close examination, this might have been a rule 10 years ago, but is it still of use today? Why not a premium version?

The real benefit of making your (or the group's) thinking rules explicit is the conversations that follow. People start to realise that they have similar but different thinking boxes. When they are made explicit, new ideas can emerge. It's why switching your rules is a great precursor to tools like brainstorming. If you don't make them explicit you can only generate ideas within your existing thinking box.

It's also why AI can be immensely valuable. It's not bound by the same thinking box you are. AI can stretch and break free of your box.

I asked AI, 'What are the five conventions of a firm of architects?' and the response was:

- Form follows function
- Hierarchy of expertise
- Long, iterative design cycles
- The architect as the sole visionary
- Billable hours = value.

This is invaluable. If you want to know more about an industry, just ask AI what the conventions of this industry are. Then ask yourself if these are the rules you want to follow. If you are a startup, once you know the conventions, ask yourself how you can switch these. An invaluable exercise is to articulate the usual rules and the new rules, as set out in figure 11.2.

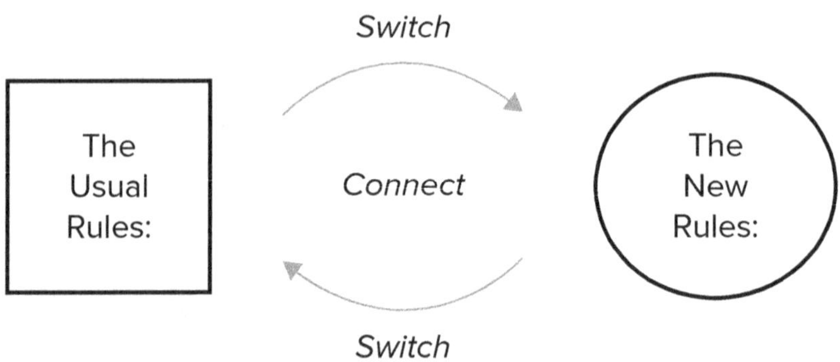

Figure 11.2 Switching your thinking rules

When you switch, challenge or break your (or others') thinking rules, you can create new results (i.e. ideas, solutions, opportunities). And, of course, try to connect the ideas from the current rules to the new rules.

Cirque du Soleil is a great example of switching the rules. It kept the core elements of a circus such as clowns and jugglers, but it changed the rules that said you need animals in a circus. It replaced these with amazing acts, music and dance to create a spell-binding experience.

But what if we go back to the architect example? I asked AI to overturn the existing conventions and it came back with:

- Switch from 'form follows function' to 'form follows feeling'.
- Switch from hierarchy to collaboration.
- Switch from long cycles to 2-minute sketch challenges.
- Switch from 'I designed this' to 'We co-created this'.
- Switch from hours to impact.

Now, I would have thought of a few of these myself, yet AI still surprised me with others that it suggested (e.g. 'form follows feeling').

My point is this. AI can help you switch your rules and in fact may be one of the best ways to do this because it has no emotional attachments to any of your thinking rules.

Changing the rules

I once facilitated a tense workshop between a major brand and a national retailer. Both teams were stuck in a negotiation gridlock.

I started the session with one sentence: 'Everything is on the table. Contributions are welcome but only if the idea benefits both parties'.

That one switch of the rules changed the tone instantly.

Rather than defending their turf, both sides (after a while) began to co-create business-building ideas that genuinely worked for both of them. One even said, 'This idea helps us, but not you—so let's scrap it'.

Later, an older executive quietly said, 'Your circuit-breaking rule change—that was the difference'.

Suggestions for switching your rules

To help you switch your rules, here are a few suggestions you can use by yourself, with others or using AI.

I have found that an ideal way to Switch your rules is to name the rule you are following.

Here are some examples:

- I have assumed...
  Switch.
  Here is a way to challenge this assumption...
- A convention in this industry is (e.g. consumers buy on quality over price).
  Switch.
  Here is a way to break free of this convention...
- I have always believed you are not interested in going to the theatre.
  Switch.
  Is this true? Would you like me to get two tickets for a show?

Notice how naming the rules often takes the pressure off. There is no right or wrong—just an attempt to make what is unseen, seen.

It often takes courage to ask the question, 'What rule am I following here?'

Here are a few other switches I have used myself or with groups and teams:

- What have I always done?
  Switch.
  What is something I have never tried before?
- What is my competition doing?
  Switch.
  What can I do differently?

Remember, your rules do not have to be logical or rational. They are rules you are following for whatever reason. Don't judge yourself. Just capture anything that might be influencing your thinking right now.

Making your current rules explicit gives you permission to talk about the unsaid. It acknowledges that rules aren't just logical—they're emotional, even cultural. And once seen, they become malleable—like clay, not concrete.

Guidelines, not rules

When you come across what you or others think of as a rule, use the word 'guideline' instead. That way it becomes less permanent and rigid in your mind. (Of course, stay within the law and always be ethical.)

> What is a thinking rule you are following right now?
> *Switch.*
> What happens when you think of it as a guideline? In the next 2 minutes, what emerges?

The great news is you can now help others to escape the often-limiting rules that restrict their life. Select one and help them challenge, stretch or break free of it. Try this with someone you know for a few minutes and see what emerges for them. Then they can go back to the current rule, if they wish. Also, you do not have to change all the rules; just throw out the ones that are no longer relevant.

WHOOP

Are you wearing a WHOOP health and performance device yet? I'm not, but my younger daughter and all of her friends are. What is the attraction, I wonder? Why have another wearable device?

Let's answer these questions using a Switch thinking lens. First, WHOOP measures everything, it seems, including:

- heart rates
- sleep patterns
- blood pressure.

It offers scores, baseline, trends and comparisons.

This is Box Mode thinking at its best. It appeals to disciple, logic, analysis, objectivity and a desire for monitoring and control. It answers the question, 'What is happening right now?'

This is half the story, I suspect.

If you stay in Box Mode, you can become obsessive and it might paradoxically lead to anxiety.

However, if you switch to Ball Mode, this information becomes a goldmine of insights. You can ask questions such as:

- That's interesting—why might that be?
- What was different yesterday, I wonder?
- Is a pattern starting to emerge?
- What might happen if I try something new?

This is classic Ball Mode thinking: curiosity, hypothesis, pattern sensing, experimentation, and so on. WHOOP viewed through this lens tries to answer different questions about meaning or insight rather than just results.

As such, perhaps the real appeal of WHOOP is that it allows you to measure and create meaning in real time. You have a tool at your disposal that gives you agency and control and can lead to a healthier, more engaging life.

Now I get it.

2-minute Switch Thinking exercise

Draw a box

This is my favourite rule-breaking exercise.

Draw a box.

Whatever you are working on or thinking about right now, draw inside this box (it can be big) as many assumptions, beliefs, conventions or expectations as you can in the next 2 minutes.

Don't filter.

There is no right or wrong. The goal is to make these explicit.

Now select one. Try to challenge, stretch or overturn this rule.

What happens?

Chapter 12

Switch your questions

Many years ago, I attended a conference on savants. These wonderful individuals often have an extraordinary ability in a specific area. One of the speakers mentioned a savant who could memorise a piece of music after only hearing it once.

I wondered, do they feel the music, does it move them or are they just repeating the music (although this is exceptional in itself)?

Some 20 years later I regret not asking this question at the time.

The message?

Don't be like me. Be more like Sir Richard Branson, for example, who is always asking questions of everyone he meets.

In short, questions are a way to connect with a subject, person or situation. It's a way to better understand what is happening and why, and as we will explore it's a powerful source of insight and creativity.

Questions that stop you (and others)

Have you ever been in a meeting, presentation or classroom and someone asks an unexpected, insightful question?

I have.

The room goes quiet as people ponder what was just asked. In my experience, what follows is a burst of creative energy. Yet this experience is rare.

But imagine if you could ask such a question on demand. Wouldn't that be amazing?

What's stopping you?

Part of the problem is that we have been taught in our education and professional lives that asking the right questions will lead to the right answers. And the reverse is also true: we believe that the right answers arrived because we asked the right questions. This is a powerful form of circular logic.

Conventional tools such as the '5Ws and H' (i.e. who, what, when, where, why and how) are inherently Box Mode. These types of questions organise, clarify, provide a structure and can close in on potential answers. They narrow the focus, identify boundaries, reinforce the current assumptions, give you confidence you are solving the right problem and determine who is responsible and what the budget, timeline and next steps might be.

Box Mode questions work beautifully when you need logic, structure or decision making but they narrow rather than expand the solution space.

These types of questions work well in a stable, rule-based world. But in today's volatile, uncertain, complex and ambiguous world, that old model breaks down.

There often is no single right answer — only better questions that lead to more meaningful exploration. For example, consider the problem of the increasing incidence of anxiety in our younger generation. Is it social media, or political uncertainty, a lack of a career path, threats from AI? There is no single, right answer. Perhaps just better questions.

> What's a question you wish you'd asked? What stopped you? Why?

Another aspect of asking Box Mode questions is that in many professional cultures (especially consulting, law, finance), knowing the answer is associated with competence, confidence and control. However, with AI, for example, it's not just answers that matter, it's the quality of your questions and your ability to stay open when you don't know.

With AI it's the originality and creativity of your prompts that can make a real difference. It's why I am suggesting a new category of prompt imagining that can work alongside prompt engineering.

Asking Box Mode questions also rarely leads to any sort of competitive edge.

Why?

Often your competitors are asking the same questions as you. This means you are all looking in the same place for the answers. Why not look in a different place for more innovative answers?

Perhaps we all need to switch from 'I should know the answer' to 'This is a chance to ask a better question'.

I call this 'Switch your questions'.

I am suggesting that, for most problems, issues or situations you pause for just a few moments and focus on the questions you are asking rather than the answers you seek.

It's a paradox that if you want to create breakthrough answers or solutions start first with the questions you are asking.

For example:

Pause: I am often asked why change is so hard.
Switch: What if we switched this question and asked how we can make change incredibly easy?
Play: This might lead you to consider introducing change to your team, classroom or home that is fun, simple, short, reversible and safe. You might ask your kids what change they would like to make on the weekends.

It's a voyage of discovery to find more insightful questions.

But why focus on questions rather than directly on answers?

I have found in my Switch Thinking workshops that asking the same questions nearly always leads to the same answers. For example, 'How can I improve my AI skills?' is a legitimate question but it rarely leads to an imaginative response.

Asking instead, 'How can I make AI my creative partner?' is a very different type of question. And it might lead to more interesting responses.

Notice what has happened?

You switched from Box Mode Questions to Ball Mode ones. And by doing so you opened your mind to more creative ideas. This is illustrated in figure 12.1.

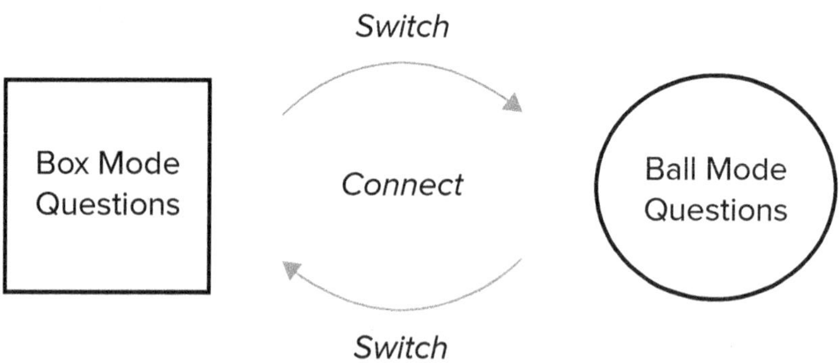

Figure 12.1 Switching your questions

If you are thinking of making a change in your life, ask yourself 'What's a fun question?' Or an absurd question. Perhaps a novel question.

Do this in 2 minutes so you get in the habit of asking questions without filtering.

What is a Ball Mode question?

A Ball Mode question is one that opens rather than closes, surprises rather than confirms and invites imagination rather than judgement. It's the kind of question that creates mental space, sparks wonder and often leads to insights you didn't expect.

For example:

- What would I do if I weren't trying to be reasonable?
- What would make this fun instead of hard?
- What would I do if I knew I could not fail?
- What if I started again, not with what's possible but with what's magical?
- What would a wild, ridiculous, beautiful solution look like here?

In short:

Ball Mode questions don't just solve a problem in a new way — they shift the way you think about it.

A Ball Mode question is one that is new, challenging and often emotional.

For example, consider these Box Mode, then Ball Mode, questions:

- What's a question a competitor might ask?
  Switch.
  What's a question a startup might ask?
- What's a frequently asked question?
  Switch.
  What's a question no-one is asking?
- What's a safe question?
  Switch.
  What's a scary question?

Can you see that these Ball Mode questions open your mind to new possibilities? If you get stuck, ask AI to help you.

When you switch from answers to questions, you leap from control to curiosity, from certainty to discovery and from judgement to exploration.

Most of all you switch from confirming your knowledge or expertise to being open to new possibilities, learning and growth.

> What challenge are you struggling with now? Pause and ask yourself, what are two Box Mode questions, then two Ball Mode questions? Don't filter; try to develop the four questions in 2 minutes or less.

The key in this exercise is to focus on questions only; try to fight your natural tendency to answer these. That is stage two. Then play with the answers to these questions. Aim for insight rather than accuracy, being different rather than being right.

Let's consider a challenge.

How can I reduce my anxiety when I meet new people?

Here are some Ball Mode questions you can ask yourself (or bounce off a friend):

- When have I ever felt confident — even briefly — and what made it happen?
- What's a playful or surprising way I could break the ice?
- What if they are as nervous as I am? How can I help them?

These types of questions open space for possibility, self-compassion, agency and creativity. The key point is that unlike Box Mode questions there is no right or wrong Ball Mode question.

When you switch your questions, you can ask anything you wish, at any time, for any reason.

The brain science

Asking Ball Mode questions works with the way the brain networks interact.

When you introduce a surprising or unrelated question, your salience network registers this difference and triggers your Ball Mode (i.e. DMN). This, as we have discussed, is your home of creativity and imagination.

Asking a novel question also disrupts your habitual neural patterns, which can lead to more divergent thinking, the use of metaphors and intuition. Think of it like a thought detour that suddenly leads back to the main road with a better view.

In short, asking a non-linear question of yourself, others or AI greatly increases the chances of developing a non-linear answer. This is incredibly powerful in those moments that matter.

Which brings me to an even bigger switch-your-question idea.

Random questions using AI

I love this idea as it not only opens your mind in the most magical way, but it works perfectly with AI. As the name suggests, you ask random questions about the challenge you are working on. The goal is to expand not just your problem space but your solution space.

Here is a real example of this idea. It's counter-intuitive, but stay with me: it will be worth it.

Here is challenge that I created:

What is my next career move?

I then asked AI this random question:

How do bees fly?

Why did I ask this question? It was completely random; it just came into my head. At first, this seems absurd. It's prompt imagining at play.

In this interaction I have indicated my AI response and my reaction as my thinking was challenged and opened to the challenge, 'What is my next career move?'

AI: Bees aren't aerodynamically 'meant' to fly, yet they do.

This made me consider that maybe I don't need to wait until everything is perfectly aligned in my life to make a move. I can act even if it doesn't seem like I should be able to.

AI: Bees navigate using collective memory and instinct.

This challenged me: I could reflect on what I've instinctively been drawn to over time — even if it hasn't made sense on paper. What is my version of 'instinct'?

AI: Bees constantly switch roles in the hive — from nurse to worker to forager to guard.

I wondered, maybe my next move isn't permanent. Like a bee, I could try on a new role temporarily. I don't need a forever plan — I need a next step.

AI: Bees create immense value (honey, pollination) by doing small, repetitive acts.

My reaction: perhaps I should focus less on a giant leap and more on building momentum through consistent micro-actions.

I was genuinely surprised and delighted by this series of responses and interactions with and from AI. What started out as a thought experiment turned into a completely new insight.

Asking random questions is the ideal way to take advantage of the processing power and capability of AI to make novel connections. And what's more, it happened in a few moments. I can reject some or all of these responses but asking a random question unlocked an array of new possibilities to the challenge. 'What is my next career move?'

In this new world, AI led by you can handle the known and explore the unknown. Together, you can create a switching ecosystem where logic and imagination, facts and wonder, partner in possibility.

The question generator and receiver cycle

Asking a Box Mode or Ball Mode question is often just the start of an interaction. When you are working in a group or team, how that question is received can impact any future collaboration. For example, a team leader can receive a naïve question from a junior team member and dismiss it instantly or they can see it as what it is: a beautiful reminder of what they don't see anymore.

Asking a Ball Mode question means nothing if the receiver is not open to hearing the answer. Switching your thinking involves switching your attention, from preparing your response to fully listening. The real power of a question lies not just in asking it but in pausing long enough to let the answer breathe.

Encouraging Ball Mode questions leads to a positive cycle of more insightful Ball Mode questions, which can lead to greater creativity, collaboration, exploration and risk-taking.

A final question:

Why switch your thinking?

Switch.

Why not switch your thinking?

Being able to switch your thinking boosts your confidence, develops a life skill and enhances your creativity, energy and agility. And it gives you a simple, practical and empowering toolkit to help everyone around you be at their best.

2-minute Switch Thinking exercise

Work with a partner and select a challenge that you are both struggling with.

In the next 2 minutes each of you generates nine questions about this challenge. There is no right or wrong question to ask. Avoid the temptation of answering any of the questions.

Now swap lists with your partner.

Select a question you don't know the answer to. They do the same. Have fun, play with your response.

What new possibilities emerge?

Conclusion: The future belongs to switch thinkers

Many years ago, I went over to my parents' place for a Sunday roast. Just before we sat down, Dad suggested we go for a walk. As we strolled, he turned to me and asked, 'Are you happy, son?'

I paused, then answered honestly, 'No. I'm miserable'.

At the time, I had been separated from my partner and didn't know what to do next.

Dad didn't lecture me. He just replied, 'If that's the case, why don't you do something about it?'

That question — asked at just the right time, from a place of love — switched my thinking. It helped me stop procrastinating, stop worrying about what others might think and start reclaiming control of my life. I had gone from stuck to unstuck in minutes!

Within a week, I had a heartfelt conversation with my ex-partner and we both agreed to move in different directions. She has since met a wonderful partner. And I've now been happily married with my soulmate for years.

That was an unexpected 'switch your thinking' moment. It was my dad at his best: insightful, kind and loving. It was brief, simple, yet powerful because it changed how I thought, felt and what I did.

It was a moment shared between my dad and me that helped me regain my agency.

In these moments a small switch in thinking, even for just a few minutes, can have a potentially big impact on you and others. The switch need only be 2 minutes or less—just enough time for you to switch from Box Mode to Ball Mode to open yourself to new possibilities or to switch from Ball Mode to Box Mode to evaluate, prioritise and accelerate progress.

This model of switching between Box and Ball Modes in bursts of 2 minutes is a new just-in-time way to create, solve, imagine and move forward when you are stuck. In these 2 minutes you learn by doing—or more accurately, by switching.

The ability to switch your thinking sits in the space between before and after that many other approaches miss. Coaching, mentoring, mindfulness, visualisation and journalling, to name a few, can be effective either before or after any process, interaction or conversation. They can help you prepare and reflect, learn and grow.

But what happens when you are faced with a room full of leaders, students or work colleagues who are looking at you to help them right now?

In these moments, when it feels like everything is on the line (it's often not, by the way, but it can feel this), being able to switch your thinking could help you and the group see a situation in a new way, ask a question that stimulates a new wave of discussion or use a metaphor that unlocks new insights and possibilities.

Switch Thinking is like a game of chess where you unexpectedly use your knight to jump over other pieces, which can place you in a winning position. The option was always there but you had not seen it before. Some people call this a moment of genius, but you realise that it's a skill (like playing chess) you can develop with practice. It's not magic, but it sometimes feels like it.

One more time: What is Switch Thinking?

I have defined Switch Thinking in the introduction as: *the skill of knowing when — and how — to change the way you think.*

This is such a simple yet powerful idea. You can learn to switch your thinking when you need to, from what I call Box Mode to Ball Mode via a series of 6 switches and prompts. It's deliberate and can be used to respond to and/or create change, learning and growth.

You decide.

The most exciting insight for me is that Switch Thinking is a skill such as learning a musical instrument or another language. These skills, like Switch Thinking, can enrich your life. This means you can practise, develop and improve this skill with the right tools, encouragement and usage. And most importantly it can be taught to others.

Most people are surprised by the extent to which they can control or influence their thinking. This is such an empowering insight. You do not have to think the same way you always have. You have agency; you can change.

I have also suggested a 3-step PSP process (i.e. Pause — Switch — Play). These trigger words can help you, in most situations, to create the awareness and space to change how you think, feel and act in any situation.

To help you switch your thinking I have outlined two modes of thinking (Box Mode and Ball Mode) based on the latest brain science. I have used these as descriptive metaphors that make the idea of thinking more accessible and useful, and encourage movement rather than a type of person. Much like being able to be in work mode and holiday mode. You often only need to switch for only a few minutes to make a big, positive impact on any situation at work, home and everywhere in between.

I have also outlined 6 switches that anyone can use, anytime, for any situation. These can be used in any order and any number of times. The switches provide a way to interrupt your default way of thinking and to explore a new direction and see what happens. If it does not work out, you can switch back to your original way of thinking.

I have found that switching your thinking can be developed, practised and communicated to others with ease. It's fast, intuitive and empowering and mirrors how your brain networks operate.

The beauty of Switch Thinking is that it empowers you to switch to a new mode without judgement for just a few minutes. You can then see the situation differently with greater energy and confidence. You can master the moment rather than the moment mastering you.

This Switch Thinking approach is needed even more in a continually changing, uncertain world where noise is increasing and attention spans are decreasing. This increasingly means that individual and collective moments matter. And in these important moments you need to be at your best—not perfect but able to lift your thinking performance to meet the challenge.

The applications for Switch Thinking are endless. You recognise that moving away from the tried and true, or what has worked in the past, to a new approach is liberating and empowering. Even if it is only for a few minutes, it's enough to refresh and reenergise you or others. This is where the magic happens. It is in these moments that you can create a big positive impact.

As my example with my dad illustrated, a switch of thinking had an exponential impact on my life (very big, in other words). It was not a linear process where one unit of effort equals one unit of change. When you switch your thinking, you can change what you see, how you feel and what you do.

Imagine the compound effect of switching your thinking starting today and then using it tomorrow and the next day.

Here's an example.

Let's imagine you have helped your son or daughter resolve a situation they were having with a friend at university or at school. Their response when they come home is joyful. Thank you, they say. Now you have role-modelled a switch in thinking that they might then copy and use by themselves and with their friends. You also feel energised because of your kid's success.

Another example:

At work, you face a situation where your immediate team leader is ignoring your efforts. You switch your thinking: why are they doing this? Perhaps they, too, are under pressure. You now have a clearer understanding of the situation and, rather than ruminate, you switch to action. You decide in a respectful, specific way to bring this lack of appreciation to their attention. They thank you.

Can you see how a series of positive Switch Thinking experiences grows? It's empowering. Your impact is spreading far and wide through the power of helping people think in a different way. This is sustainable, transferable and has a multiplier effect. It reminds me of those funny videos where there are 1000 mouse traps and one ping pong ball is thrown in? Eventually, all the traps go off in a mighty crescendo.

This is the big switch.

You are switching from creating an individual positive impact to a collective movement. You are role-modelling a different, more empowering and collaborative way to help others in 2 minutes or less. This idea of a collective movement is captured in figure C.1 (overleaf).

And this can happen with one small switch in how we think, which can lead to a change in how we feel and what we do.

For example:

You can see Christians or Muslims.

Switch.

You can see good people throughout the world with a rich array of belief systems.

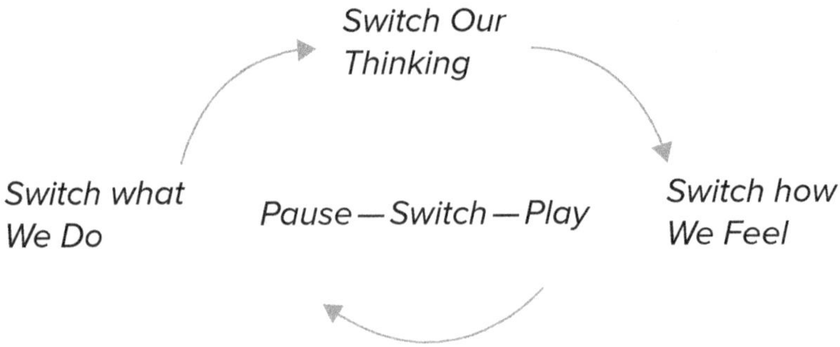

Figure C.1 The collective impact of a switch in thinking

The first thinking pattern reinforces difference and for some people distrust and suspicion. When you switch to a different way of thinking you realise that we have much more in common than what separates us.

All it takes is the courage to try a small switch for the next 2 minutes. It could be a small switch in perspective, emotion or focus that can change a conversation, a classroom, a team — even a life.

In these 2-minute switch moments you can feel more energised, liberated and empowered. When you do this once, you are more likely to seize the next moment ... and the next.

These series of 2-minute switches ensure that making a bigger change feels less overwhelming. It's just the moment in front of you. You can pause and then switch. And when you switch it need only be for 2 minutes or less. You are building a switch thinking capability step by step: one switch thinking experience at a time.

And once you start seeing these switch moments ... you start seeing them everywhere.

Switch Thinking at its heart is energising, imaginative and playful. Switching from Box Mode to Ball Mode, for example, gives you and others permission to have fun, play, take risks and explore the unknown, realising that you can easily switch back in a few minutes.

What might Beyoncé do?

Switch…

Or, how might Shaquille O'Neal approach this challenge?

By switching, you can realise your full thinking potential.

The next big switch: Individual × collective thinking

We used to believe that thinking was an individual activity. This was reinforced by images of (mostly) men deep in thought in their studio or laboratory. This is best exemplified by The Thinker sculpture by Auguste Rodin, a solitary man immersed in his thoughts.

Now thinking has changed as most work is carried out in teams via meetings, shared documents, presentations and the like. And yet, there are few thinking tools specifically designed for groups and teams—although brainstorming is one. This tool was developed by advertising executive Alex F. Osborn almost 100 years ago as a way for groups to generate new ideas. It is very popular and yet there are many criticisms of this approach: the extroverts dominate, individual loafing, production blocking, it takes time and the fear of judgement, to name a few.

It's another reason why I am excited by the potential of Switch Thinking. You can use it by yourself and in a group, it takes only a few minutes and it gives everyone a shared language (e.g. 'Why don't we switch to Ball Mode and see what happens?'). It also gives permission for some participants to be in Box Mode and others to be in Ball Mode at the same time, then interact, connect and perhaps switch modes.

The focus is on modes, not people.

The challenge is not about access to information or idea generation anymore; this is well covered by AI. It's knowing when to switch and with whom. And most importantly, it's about being able to switch during a presentation, interview, meeting or conversation. The moments that really make a difference in your day.

That's the missing skill.

This is the new territory of Switch Thinking.

For example, you have received an unexpected new job offer and the recruiter wants a response quickly.

You start in Box Mode.

What is the salary? Working hours? You check on social media for any comments. You do some background checks with AI and ask for some industry projections.

Now switch to Ball Mode. You are now looking at social media, or perhaps contacting past employees to help you answer such questions as:

- What is the culture like?
- Are their values aligned with yours?
- What is their purpose?

In this example, you are using the different modes of thinking to full effect, amplified by AI. You are switching between head and heart; human capability and intuition, and AI processing.

Switch Thinking is, I believe, the key skill that allows individual, collective and AI-augmented thinking to work together rather than compete. And the impact is multiplied.

It really is the future.

Is there anything you cannot switch?

This is such an interesting question. Politicians criticise their opponents when they change their mind. It's apparently a sign of weakness or of lacking moral substance. What happens, therefore, is that many politicians or leaders cling to their original positions despite changing circumstances.

And yet we do need our leaders to be unchanging in some areas and open to change in others.

So how to navigate this minefield (perhaps it's a mind field?). One way is to separate your thinking into a core and an outer ring. Your core is your values, principles, vision and purpose, which should not be changed without careful reflection.

But then you have your outer ring, which can be changed. This might include your assumptions, attitudes, beliefs, theories, questions, perspectives, language, models and conventions.

It might also include the people you follow, books you read and videos you watch. These can be challenged, and indeed switched, to help you adapt to a change in a situation, problem or opportunity. This two layered model is illustrated in figure C.2.

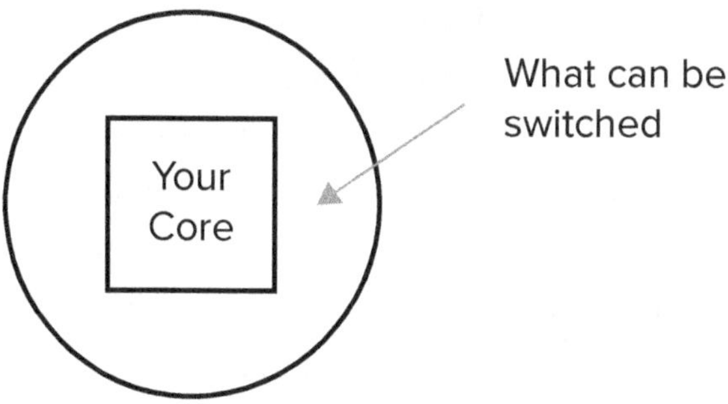

Figure C.2 **What is core and what can be changed?**

> In the next 2 minutes outline what is core in your life. What can be switched?

This twin dynamic model suggests that a Switch Thinking framework is both flexible and focused. You can retain your core *and* be prepared to let go — or at least have your thinking challenged. This framework is both disruptive and respectful.

I expect the world to change at an accelerated pace. Consider the threats and opportunities of AI as but one example. This can feel exhausting. What I have tried to do with Switch Thinking is to give you a way to enjoy this adventure.

My key message is this: You have a choice. In a rapidly changing world you can learn to change how you think, feel and act via Switch Thinking. Or risk falling behind by sticking to increasingly rigid patterns.

A thought exercise

Let's imagine two scenarios: a life without Switch Thinking and one with it.

A life *without* Switch Thinking could mean that you cannot escape the way you have always thought, felt and behaved. You believe that you cannot change as this is just the way you are. Your world is often black and white. Most change is scary because it is not easy for you to adapt. You often get stuck in one way of looking at situations, people and relationships and under pressure you revert to what has worked in the past regardless of what is happening in the moment before you.

A life *with* Switch Thinking is a life filled with colour. You can see new perspectives, possibilities and opportunities quickly. You tend to be more open to changing situations, challenges and relationships. You feel more empowered and have greater choice, control and agency. You understand and connect to other people's ideas, beliefs and experiences rather than feeling threatened by them. AI, even with its limitations, is a source of stimulus, learning and growth.

Which life do you want to live?

A final word

Years ago, after long days in a corporate job, I would walk into my home exhausted. I needed some time to download but my kids wanted to give their dad a big hug. My tiredness clashed with their excitement. Sometimes tears followed.

One day, I paused.

I switched my thinking to seeing the situation through my kids' eyes.

This switch made these moments the best part of my day.

Being able to switch your thinking means that you don't have to wait for the right moment, people or place. You are accessing your brain networks and moving between these depending on the situation or your need.

The great news is you can switch your thinking in just a few minutes, and it builds on what you are already doing but perhaps have not yet realised you are doing.

When you have experienced the power of a small switch in thinking — in how you think, feel and act — you gain more confidence and want to do this again and again. This creates a positive, ever-increasing cycle of impact. You use Switch Thinking by yourself, with others and with AI in a more creative, productive and collaborative way.

My hope is that a small switch in thinking can lead to a big difference in you, your team, community and society.

2-minute Switch Thinking exercise

Try a smaller switch, then a bigger one

I have found that when you are introducing Switch Thinking to others it is often beneficial if you start with a smaller switch first. This helps them get used to the idea and feel more confident before you try stretching their minds by introducing a bigger switch.

For example:

Usual: What is the customer perspective?

Smaller switch: What is a startup perspective?

Bigger switch: What might a clown perspective be?

This graduated approach helps people get used to the idea of switching in a safer, more empowering way.

Get in touch

For more information on Switch Thinking, visit:

- switchthinking.net
- drkenhudson.com
- View: youtube.com/@switchthinking
- Email: ken@drkenhudson.com
- Call: 61 2 412323824

Keep switching, it's your hidden power.

Acknowledgements

A big thank to the following people in particular who expanded and sharpened my ideas over many years:

Phil Baker, Ben Berger, Pilita Clark, Christopher Cosier, Mark Cripps, Charlotte Denman, Amanda Digby, Stephen Digby, Eelsha Dixon, Michael Doyle, Heinz Fickler, Carolyn Fickler, Anne Gately, Ben Holgate, Greg Joffe, Justin Kirkwood, Paul Leinberger, Sally Neighbour, D'arne O'Neill, Greg O'Neill, Katie O'Neill, Mark Preddey, Virginia Preddey, Kristin Sinclair, Peter Wilson and all the gang at Clodeli where I often did my best thinking.

I would also like to thank the people from Wiley, in particular Jordan for believing in the book, Chris for making it happen and Renee for promoting it.

Most of all I have (mostly) enjoyed the feedback from Molly Hudson and Margot O'Neill. They always made my work better.

Appendix A: Switch Thinking prompts for neurodiverse minds

In the next few pages, I have outlined several prompts that wonderful neurodiverse minds might find helpful. I often read about the deficits of having an ADHD mind, yet not as much on the powerful advantages.

Recent research has suggested that people who are ADHD can often solve problems with spontaneous, intuitive leaps. Other people who are very strong analytically tend to solve problems effectively in a more structured way. Most of us (myself included), who are in the middle, are not quite as adept at creating breakthrough solutions. Switch Thinking offers a fast, easy and practical way to access the best of both worlds (analysis and spontaneous insight). In other words, it helps you switch and use both ways of thinking when you need them.

Using the 6 switches

These are just suggestions, but they illustrate how each of the 6 switches can incorporate the 'switch off & switch on' structure.

Not every prompt will work every time — that's the point. Try one, see what happens and switch again.

Remember: each switch only takes 2 minutes!

1 Switch your perspective

Switch off: Being the visionary
Switch on: Be an angel investor. What are three tangible reasons why someone should invest in your idea?
Switch off: Being a chef who is creating a brand-new dish
Switch on: Be a novice cook in the kitchen who wants to follow a step-by-step recipe.
Switch off: Being a conductor.
Switch on: Be a violinist who wants to play the notes as they are written down.

2 Switch your focus

Switch off: Worrying about what you are not good at
Switch on: Focus on what makes you awesome — every day!
Switch off: Focusing on what's left to do
Switch on: Focus on what has already been done.
Switch off: Talking too much
Switch on: Listening (like an interviewer): What are they saying that makes me curious? How can I respond to show I was listening?

3 Switch on your imagination

Switch off: Creating the perfect solution
Switch on: Studying my competitors: What can I learn, borrow or adapt?
Switch off: Dreaming.
Switch on: Talking to some potential customers or users and obtaining real feedback about my new idea.
Switch off: Imagining your next big idea
Switch on: Making my current idea 10× more practical, easy and simple.

4 Switch your emotions

Switch off: Ruminating on how you are feeling now
Switch on: Draw how you would like to feel.
Switch off: Feeling bored
Switch on: Play with your small, coloured ball. Squeeze it; throw it from one hand to the other.
Switch off: Feeling blue
Switch on: Select another colour. What does orange feel like? Or green?

5 Switch your rules

Switch off: Working on your project in a logical way
Switch on: Start thinking and working on any part of the project that interests you.
Switch off: Sitting still doing the same thing for hours
Switch on: Get up and move, listen to music, go for a walk.
Switch off: You need to adhere to a strict deadline
Switch on: Fun, spontaneous deadlines (e.g. what is one part of this assignment I can knock off in the next 2 minutes?).

6 Switch your questions

Switch off: What's the entire plan?
Switch on: What's the very next step?
Switch off: How do I avoid making mistakes on the entire project?
Switch on: How can I develop systems to help me not make a mistake in the next hour?
Switch off: How do I stay focused?
Switch on: What's the most exciting part I can do first?
Switch off: Listening to the noise
Switch on: What's important?

• • •

I have found that the 'switch off and switch on' framework can help you when you are feeling stuck, overwhelmed or just need an energy boost. It gives you a simple (but not simplistic), actionable instruction (think Ikea instructions for your mind).

It's an easy and empowering way to help you bypass the sometime clutter of your inner world that can lead to inaction.

In addition, the 2-minute time frame helps you kickstart any project without worrying about the outcome or potentially failing.

The 2-minute 'switch off and switch on' framework is a killer app for your beautiful mind that I hope you use, enjoy and find it helpful.

More Switch Thinking ideas

Here are some other suggestions for using the Switch Thinking framework. You don't need to follow these in order. Pick one and try it, then select another and see what happens.

Pause

Ask yourself, 'What is the situation in front of me?'

Then ask, 'What mode is the most helpful here? Is that the mode I am in right now?' If not, then switch to the mode that is best suited to the situation for just 2 minutes. You can always switch back. For example, if you need to hand in an assignment by the end of the week, what mode might help you the most? (Hint: Box Mode)

The simple act of pausing can raise your awareness of what mode you are in and how to adapt to any situation.

Carry a switch ball with you

It can be in your bag, on your desk and at home — take it everywhere with you It's a powerful, tactile and visual reminder of Ball Mode. If you can, also carry a fun, small squeezy box to remind you to switch to Box Mode when you need to.

Play with either: when you need to focus, pick up your squeezy box; if you need to create, start playing with your ball. This physical switching (I have found) can help you switch your thinking in a fast and easy way. Remember: there is no good or bad mode, just what works in the moment in front of you.

Keep a small reminder on your desk

Place a sign on your desk at home and/or work that reads 'Switch off & switch on' to remind you of the Switch Thinking framework. Use it all the time for those quick sprints of energy and creativity. You can switch on or off at any time for a few minutes and see what emerges. Perhaps more structure when you switch on Box Mode and new ideas when you switch on Ball Mode.

Place a die on your desk

It's physical and it's a reminder of the 6 switches. Allocate one side to each switch. Roll the die and use that switch for a few minutes. Go with the flow! I love the randomness and playful nature of this approach. It has always surprised me what turns up when I break my default thinking patterns.

Buy a 2-minute timer

It could be a small hourglass, a kitchen timer or use your phone's stopwatch. The physical act of turning it on or pressing a button can help you switch on for the task. It provides you with a visual and auditory cue that reinforces the time-bound nature of the sprint, helping to keep your mind on track and prevent the task from ballooning into something overwhelming.

Keep a switch journal

Why don't you keep a simple, dedicated notebook for documenting the results of each switch? The physical journal wouldn't be a detailed log; rather, it would be a place to quickly jot down what you were able to 'create, feel or do' in your next 2-minute sprint (of course, you could use a digital record but writing it down might be slower but more meaningful). This creates a tangible record of small victories, which builds momentum and reinforces a sense of accomplishment.

Consider how far you can travel in 2 minutes

Just make a start on one thing. In 2 minutes a top-class female runner can run 800 metres. How far can you run on one issue, task or problem in the next 2 minutes? Don't stop, hesitate or second guess yourself. Just go as fast as you can on an assignment, project or 'to-do' list. You can always switch back to Box Mode and check your actions, suggestions or ideas.

In summary:

- Pause
- Pick one switch or prompt
- Play for 2 minutes
- Pause
- Switch back if you wish—you decide!

Appendix B: Prompting AI in Box Mode and Ball Mode

In Switch Thinking there are two complementary modes of Thinking. These are called Box Mode and Ball Mode.

Box Mode is structured, logical and grounded.

Ball Mode is imaginative, open and sometimes surprising.

You can use these two modes when working with AI. All you need to do is instruct AI on which mode to use.

Here is one way to do this.

- *The AI Box Mode prompt:* AI, please switch to Box Mode. Think in a structured, logical way. Focus on facts, steps and feasibility.
- *The AI Ball Mode prompt:* AI, please switch to Ball Mode. Be open, playful and imaginative. Explore unexpected possibilities, consider different perspectives and question the usual rules.

Switching between modes

The real magic, I have found, is when you switch back and forth between these two modes. There is no right or wrong way to do this. You can instruct your AI to start in either mode.

Here is a real example I developed:

AI, I want to develop a new video on Instagram using chess as a powerful way to illustrate the experience of Switch Thinking.

AI, in Box Mode can you give me one example of how to do this?

AI responded with the idea of a video of me playing both sides of a chess board. This represents the idea of how a simple switch of a position or role can help you see a situation differently.

Next, I asked:

AI, in Ball Mode, can you give me a different idea?

AI responded with the idea of having each of the pieces talking to me and giving advice as to the next move. This illustrates a switch in perspective.

Lastly I asked:

AI, can you switch back to Box Mode. Out of these two concepts can you evaluate in terms of impact, cost and timing. (In this case, AI suggested the talking pieces one as the winner.)

As this example illustrates, you can instruct AI to use and respond either in Box Mode or Ball Mode. By doing so, you will obtain quite different responses. The true potential of AI is achieved by using both of these modes and switching between them. Remember, you are in the driving seat.

References

Amabile T. & Kramer S. (2011). *The progress principle: Using Small wins to ignite joy, engagement and creativity at work,* Harvard Business Review Press.

Bar, M. (2022). *Mindwandering: How it can improve your mood and boost your creativity,* Bloomsbury.

Barker, J.A. (1993). *Paradigms: The business of discovering the future,* Harper Business.

Beilock, S. (2011). *Choke: Use the secrets of your brain to succeed when it matters most,* Melbourne University Press.

Berger, W.A. (2014). *A more beautiful question,* Bloomsbury US.

Bergren, M., Cox, M. & Detmar, J. (2002) *Improvise this-how to think on your feet so you don't fall on your face,* Hyperion.

Berns, G. 2008. *Iconoclast: A neuroscientist reveals how to think differently,* Harvard Business School Publishing.

Chen, Q., Kenett, Y.N., Cui, Z. et al. (2025). Dynamic switching between brain networks predicts creative ability, *Communications Biology, 8*, 54.

Clear, J. (2018). *Atomic habits, tiny changes: Remarkable results,* Random House.

Csikszentmihalyi, M. (2008). *Flow: The psychology of optimal experience,* Harper Collins.

De Bono, E. (1992). *Serious creativity: Using the power of lateral thinking* to create new ideas, Harper Collins.

De Bono, E. (2007). *How to have creative ideas,* Ebury Publishing.

Doidge, N. (2007). *The brain that changes itself, Scribe* Publications.

Dweck, C. S. (2006). *Mindset: Changing the way you think to fulfil your potential,* Random House.

Eapen, T. T., Finkenstadt, D.J. & Folk, J. (2023). How generative AI can augment human creativity, *Harvard Business Review,* July-August.

Edelman S. (2002). *Change your thinking,* ABC Books.

Ericsson, A. (2016). *Peak: Secrets from the new science of expertise,* The Bodley Head.

Fogg, B.J. (2019). *Tiny habits: The small changes that change everything,* Virgin Books.

Fox, E. (2022). *Switchcraft: Harnessing the power of mental agility to transform your life,* Hodder & Stoughton.

Gleick, J. (1987). *Chaos: Making a new science,* William Heinemann.

Goleman, D. (2005). *Emotional intelligence: Why it can matter more than IQ,* Bantam Publishing.

González-Díaz, J., Gossner, O. & Rogers, B. W. (2012). Performing best when it matters most: Evidence from professional tennis, *Journal of Economic Behavior & Organization, 84*(3), 767–781.

Grandin, T. (2022). *Visual thinking,* Ebury Publishing.

Grant, A. (2021), *Think again: The power of knowing what you don't know,* WH Allen.

Grazer, B. & Fishman, C. (2015). *A curious mind: The secret to a bigger life,* Simon & Schuster.

Heath, C. & Heath, D. (2010). *Switch: How to change things when change is hard,* Random House.

Hewitt-Gleeson, M. (1991). *Software for the brain,* Wrightbooks.

Hudson, K. (2007), *The Idea Generator: Tools for Business Growth,* Sydney, Allen & Unwin.

Hudson, K. (2010). *Speed Thinking: How to thrive in a time poor world,* Allen & Unwin.

Jay, M. (2024). *The twenty-something treatment: A revolutionary remedy for young adult mental health,* 4th Estate.

Jebelli, J. (2025). *The brain at rest: Why doing nothing can change your life,* Transworld Publishers.

Kaufman, S. B. & Gregoire, C. G. (2015). *Wired to create: Imaginative play,* Perigee.

Kotler, S. (2021). *The art of impossible: A peak performance primer,* Harper Collins.

Kounios, J. & Beeman M. (2015). *The Eureka Factor: Aha moments, creative insight, and the brain,* Random House.

Kross, E. & Ayduk, O. (2017). Self-distancing: Theory, research, and current Directions. *Advances in Experimental Social Psychology, 55,* 81–136.

Lotto, B. (2017). *Deviate: The science of seeing differently,* Weidenfeld & Nicolson.

Lu, J.G., Akinola, M. & Mason, M.F. (2017). Switching on creativity: Task switching can increase creativity by reducing cognitive fixation, *Organisational Behavior and Human Decision Process, 139*(C), 63–75.

Lu, J.G., Sun, S., Zhuyi, A., Foo, M. & Zhou, J. (2026). Why AI boosts creativity for some employees but not others, *Harvard Business Review,* 7 January.

Luchini, A., Volle, E., & Beaty, R.E. (2025). The role of the default mode network in creativity, *Current Opinion in Behavioural Sciences, 65,* October, 101551.

Maisano, H., Chesebrough, C., Zhang, F., Daly, B., Beeman, M. & Kounios, J. (2026). ADHD symptom magnitude predicts creative problem-solving performance and insight versus analysis solving modes, *Personality and Individual Differences, 254.*

Martin, R. (2007). *The opposable mind: How successful leaders win through integrative thinking,* Harvard Business School Publishing.

Meevissen, Y.M., Peters, M.L. & Alberts, H.J. (2011). Become more optimistic by imagining a best possible self: Effects of a two-week intervention. *Journal of Behavior Therapy and Experimental Psychiatry, 42*(3), 371–378.

Mlodinow, L. (2018). *Elastic: The power of flexible thinking,* Allen Lane.

Monib, W.K., Qazi A. & Apong, R.A. (2024). Microlearning beyond boundaries: A systematic review and a novel framework for improving learning outcomes. *Heliyon, 11*(2).

Moore, M. (2024). Overcoming functional fixedness to improve problem-solving skills, *PsychCentral,* 17 September.

Morgan, G. (2006). *Images of organisations,* Sage Publications.

Oishi, S. (2025). *Life in three dimensions,* Transworld Publishers.

Rubin, R. (2023). *The creative act: A way of being,* Canongate Books.

Schön, D. (1983). *The reflective practitioner: How professionals think in action,* Temple Smith.

Seeley, W.W. (2019). The Salience Network: A neural system for perceiving and responding to homeostatic demands, *Journal of Neuroscience, 39*(50).

Sinek, S. (2009). *Start with Why: How great leaders inspire everyone to take action,* Portfolio.

Suleyman, M. (2025). *The coming wave,* Penguin Random House.

Sutton, J. & Jebelli, J. (2025). The brain is doing a lot of something when we appear to be doing nothing, *The Psychologist,* The British Psychological Society, 18 June.

Swart, T. (2019). *The source: Open your mind, change your life,* Ebury Publishing.

Tetreault, N. (2025). Creatives unlock unique brain networks: High creativity requires large-scale brain networks, *Psychology Today,* 1 April.

Thaler, R. H. & Sunstein, C. S. (2008). *Nudge: Improving decisions about health, wealth and happiness,* Penguin Group.

Toon, N. (2024). *How AI thinks: How we built it, how it can help us, and how we can control it,* Torva.

Vignola, N. (2024). *Rewire: Break the cycle, alter your thoughts and create lasting change,* Michael Joseph.

Walsh, T. (2025), *The shortest history of AI,* Black Inc.

Williams, C. (2025). How your whole imagination is conjured up from three brain processes, *New Scientist,* 28 May.

Wiseman, R. (2009). *59 Seconds: Think a little change a lot,* Pan Books.